GOOD OLD
HESSLE ROAD

STORIES OF HULL'S TRAWLING
AND COMMUNITY LIFE

by

ALEC GILL

Foreword by
ROY WOODCOCK

HUTTON PRESS
1991

Published by the Hutton Press Ltd.
130 Canada Drive, Cherry Burton, Beverley
North Humberside HU17 7SB

Printed and bound by

Clifford Ward & Co (Bridlington) Ltd.
55 West Street, Bridlington, East Yorkshire
YO15 3DZ

ISBN 1 872167 13 6

CONTENTS

DEDICATION

This book is dedicated to "STAND" —
the campaign group that wants the old lockhead
and riverside buildings preserved on
HULL'S ST.ANDREW'S FISH DOCK.
And to have them transformed into a
HERITAGE PARK
and
GARDEN OF REMEMBRANCE
to
THE LOST TRAWLERMEN OF HULL

St. Andrews Fish Dock
Heritage Park Action Group.

ACKNOWLEDGEMENTS

Betty Abel, Peter Adamson, George Andrews, Neil Armstrong, Tony & Muriel Ashton, Ethel Atkinson, Gertrude Attwood, Charles Ayre, Albert Bailey, Fred Barber, Fred Baskerville, Colin Bassett, Ron Bateman, Dennis Batty, Arthur Beal, Chris Bell, Marlene Bell, Len Berner, Pauline Bielby, Ernie Bilocca, Sheila & Paul Bloomfield, George & Enid Bone, Michael Boyd, Leo & Margaret Brown, George Bunn, Neville & Eileen Burton, Dorothy Butler, Vera Campbell, Amelia Carmichael, Louise Carr, Edith Casey, Marian & Arthur Chambers, Dennis & Wendy Chapman, Diane Chapman, Geoffrey Chapman, Elsie Chappell, Gillian Chiltern, Dorothy Chilton, Ian Church, Rose Clark, Tom Clark, George Cook, Arthur Cowan, Charles Cox, John & Marlene Crimlis, Ian Cundall, Harry Daglish, Bill Dale, Evelyn Davies, Jo de Gournai, Arthur & Margaret Denton, Grace Devine, Mavis Dick, Grace Dilcock, Annie Dixon, Joan Dobson, Doreen Dockerill, Jessie Dodson, Harry Downes, Maggie Doyle, Roy Dresser, Charles Drever, Ethel Drewery, Barbara Dunn, Audrey Dunne, Nora Dunning, Ivy Edwards, Leonard Embley, Leonard Enevoldson, John Evans, Michael & Dave Evans, Frances & Tony Farrow, Freda & Charlie Fee, Hilda Firth, Alfred Fishburn, Olive Fisher, Doreen & George Fleet, Laurie & Kathleen Forth, Bill Fox, Frank Frankland, Gilly Fraser, Jim & Elinor Fuller, Malcolm Fussey, Stan & Evelyn Futty, Albert Garton, Keith Gay, Bob Gibbins, Peggy Gibbins, Marianne Grantham, Fanny Gray, Jean Gray, Sarah Gray, Tricia & Eva Gray, Ethel Greatwood, Nancy Green, Helen Greenside, Trish Griffiths, Ron Griffiths, Jonathan Grobler, Ron Haines, Doris Hairsine, Debbie Hall, Brenda Hamer, Deborah Harraway, Hella Harris, Dennis Harrison, Millie Harrison, Harold Hartley, Catrina Hayes, Alex Henderson, Grace Hilton, Ethel Hodgkinson, Cissie Hogan, Les Hollome, Ros Holt, Maureen Hood, Liz Howell, Dick Hunter, Steve Hutchinson, Alfred Ireland, Henry & Polly Irving, Christopher Jackson, Dick & Winnie Jackson, Gloria Johnson, Eric Kendall, George Kendall, Trevor Kerwin, Chris Ketchell, Mary Kilvington, Fred & Lillian Knapp, Ken Knox, Brenda Krawczyk, Danuta Krawczyk, Graham Langton, Terry Layden, Arthur Lazenby, Edna & Frank Leake, Jack Lennard, Bill Lewis, Lilly Lewis, Ann Lightfoot, Gertrude & Frank Lindo, Charles Linford, Elsie Longbone, Alf Louth, Joseph Madden, Clara & Tom Magee, Stephen & Caroline Mahoney, Malcolm Mann, Jane Marsden, Jack Marshall, Kevin Marshall, Ian Martin, Ronald Martin, Steve Massam, Alex Marwood, Cath Matthews, Liz Meech, Norman Megginson, Pete Milsom, John Morfin, Herbert Mortimer, Judi Murden, Muriel Naylor, Billie Nelson, Alfred Newsome, Carol Newton, George Nicholson, Bill O'Pray, Gordon Ostler, Henrietta Outlaw, Charlie Partridge, Ann Pattison, Ena Pattison, Len & Dorothy Pearson, Mary Pearson, Harold & Vina Petrini, Martin Plenderleith, Elizabeth Potts, Leslie Powell, Jean Prosser, Robert & Rose Ramsbottom,

Joyce Rawding, Val Rendell, Eddie & Alice Reynolds, Sid Rhymes, Barbara Richardson, Ted & Laura Rilatt, Molly & Harry Rimmington, Terry Robins, Judy Rosindale, Bryan Rudd, Jonathan Rugman, Lily & Albert Rylett, David Saltiel, Alf Sankey, Ron Sayers, Mike Scrimshaw, John Seddom, Brenda Shaw, Roy & Lottie Shippey, Brenda Simpson, Herbert Simpson, Joy Smales, Albert Smith, Amanda Smith, Arthur Smith, Derek Smith, Mary Spaven, David Stephenson, David Stipetic, Stephen & Christina Stipetic, Eric Stone, Ernie Suddaby, Paul & Betty Swinscoe, David Tavener, Don Taylor, Doreen Taylor, John & Irene Taylor, Malcolm Thompson, Tom Thurston, Joyce Tonge, Vera Turnbull, George Turpin, Ethel Warcup, Bill Ward, Tommy & Christina Watts, Andrea Waudby, Joyce & George Waudby, Mike Waudby, Mavis & Roy Wegg, Maise Weightman, Mary Welburn, Tony & Ethel Westoby, Samantha White, Clarrie Wilcockson, Dorothy Wilkinson, Christine & Mort Williams, Robert Wise, Roy Woodcock, Phil Woods, Martin Woodward, Helen Wootten, Kitty Wordingham, Eileen Wright, John Wray, and Stanley Young.

FOREWORD
by
ROY WOODCOCK
EDITOR OF THE HULL TARGET

Alec Gill and I first met more than ten years ago. I was then the columnist *John Humber* of the Hull Daily Mail and he visited our offices in Jameson Street with a number of his photographs of Hessle Road.

Alec was studying at University in Wales, but making frequent visits back to his native Hull, where he had fallen in love with Hessle Road and the marvellous families that lived there. Every spare moment was spent photographing the people and places. He was out, literally, in all weathers, and even went on a trawling trip to take pictures.

To put it mildly, I was impressed with the results. They had that magical ingredient that makes a good photograph stand out from the ordinary. In a word, atmosphere. Perversely, so good were they, I resisted the temptation to use the odd one or two out of context, for here, I felt, were a set of pictures that helped tell the story of perhaps the city's most important community in its declining years.

The prints needed to be seen in their entirety and, thankfully, that year Alec's work was given an exhibition at the Posterngate Gallery in the city (1979). More exhibitions followed, including two in America.

Astonishingly, in recent years, Alec has discovered the power to move people with the written word as well — his 1987 book *Hessle Road* is a fitting culmination of his efforts there, incorporating a fine selection of those wonderful prints.

As the editor responsible for the launch of the Target Series of weekly newspapers in Hull last year I was absolutely delighted that, ten years on from our first meeting, I was able to involve Alec in our new newspaper from issue one. Alec had approached me earlier with the idea for what became *Hessle Road Corner* and from the discussions which followed I quickly decided here was a series that could become a favourite with the readers as we put together a package of ideas for the new publication. How right we were! From the start, these studies of people, superstitions, places and trawlers connected with the fishing industry proved a big hit. Alec's original commission to supply ten-weekly articles was twice extended and eventually the series ran for thirty-one weeks. We still have hopes of tempting him back to write more!

One way of judging its success is by quoting the response rate to Alec's articles from our readers. It brought in a bulging postbag of letters, many of which we published in the ensuing weeks. Sometimes new information was brought to light. On other occasions "facts" could be verified or put right! Rare photographs were unearthed. On one occasion, an article about the herring girls, led to a re-union between two friends who had not seen each other for more than fifty years. On another, references to "Cloggie" Walsh started a heated debate as to the exact location of his shop. Requests to supply back copies of the newspaper, so that readers could complete their "set" of Alec's articles, told us they were being collected and pasted into countless scrapbooks. Requests, there were, too, for the series to be brought out in a more permanent form.

I was delighted. therefore, when I learned of this new book *Good Old Hessle Road* and the extra information and photographs it contains. I feel honoured to be invited to contribute the foreword to this "best of" Hessle Road Corner and wish it every success.

ROY WOODCOCK
1990

Former herring girl Cissie Hogan (née Ashley – on the right) re-united with her long-lost travelling companion Kitty Ramshaw (née Elsworthy) in Hull on 25th February 1990. Kitty's daughter Brenda Hamer in Leicester was sent a copy of the **Hessle Road Corner** *articles (Nos. 9-10) and arranged a surprise meeting between the two friends. It was a 76th birthday treat for Kitty and the first time they had met in fifty-five years.*
Courtesy TARGET Series.

CHAPTER ONE

HESSLE ROAD CORNER:
THE BOOK

This book 'wanted' to be written. It has a life of its own. I 'wanted' to write a different book, but this one had other ideas.

Its publication resulted from the requests of others. The thirty-part series in the Hull *TARGET — Hessle Road Corner —* was not originally intended for book form; but, unknowingly, the series created an expectation. Readers anticipated that the stories were part of a book in preparation.

Several people suddenly began to ask about a book of the articles. I dismissed the idea because I wanted to write *Superstitions of Hull's Fishing Community.* Then, out of the blue, I got a telephone call from Lily Lewis. She is a member of the retired NALGO group I had spoken to at the Hull Guildhall. She regularly cut-out and saved the *Hessle Road Corner* articles, but commented that the newspaper pages did not keep very well. She was very positive and certain that they should be brought together into one volume. After that, I decided to put my previous plans aside (for the time being), and produce a book around the articles.

What must be stated quite clearly, however, is that this book *IS NOT* simply a re-printed copy of the initial articles. Each chapter has been extended, amended and elaborated beyond the original; and lots more photographs, with detailed captions, have been added.

A lovely aspect about doing the articles in the first place was that numerous Hessle Roaders took the trouble to contact me via the *TARGET* to add their memories and prints to what had been written. One good example is the net-braiders (Chapter Twelve). This two-part series (Nos. 2-3) generated many letters, phone calls and subsequent interviews. These enabled me to build up an even richer source of research material and better pictures of the braiders at work. Freda Fee's daughter, Maureen Hood, put me in touch with her mother. When I made contact with Freda, her first words were, "No, I don't have much to say about braiding". That was a sure sign she '*did* have lots of good things' to tell me. Freda's lively account has enriched the present work.

Likewise with the pictures. Stanley Young is just one of many kind people who loaned 'new' prints of old Hessle Road. His set not only related to the braiders, but also to the Herring Girls (Chapter Four). His mother, Jenny, worked as a braider for Gourocks Ropeworks, while her sister travelled as a herring girl between Blyth and Yarmouth in 1910.

It has been wonderful to interview so many people and, once again, I was overwhelmed by the generous spirit of the Hessle Roaders. There is something very special about their nature which probably springs from their links with Hull's fishing community and industry.

Hessle Road was the main thoroughfare and back-bone of the fishing community. People poured there from the nearby streets for their food and clothes, their work and play. In the centre of this pre-WWI print (c.1912) is the Division Road junction (to the left) which marks the Anglo-Saxon boundary of ancient Myton.
Courtesy Edna Leake.

It was the people who made Hessle Road "Good Old Hessle Road". Their personality invested the place with its magic. This between-the-wars print in Daltry Street (at the rear of the Madeley Street Public Baths) portrays character upon each face. The whole of humanity is here: from babes-in-arms to frail elderly women. This picture gives a feel of the community spirit for which Hessle Road is famous.
Courtesy Sarah Gray.

What is also beneficial for the research is that people have not been slow to point out when I got things wrong. It is essential that the record be put straight. Although it is impossible to be absolutely certain about anything; a writer has a responsibility to get things as right as humanly possible. This much is owed to future generations.

One result of all the contact, generated by the *TARGET* articles, is that the 'Acknowledgement' section of this book is quite large. In all, there are over 280 names. Some helped more than others, of course; but I am indebted to them all (hopefully, no one has been missed out!). The help some gave is perhaps not directly related to the current book, but may be crucial in years to come for future research. Nonetheless, because they took the trouble to help me at this time, I feel that some form of public 'thank you' is appropriate while the contact is still fresh.

So far then, I have related some of the background to how this book was formed. What of its contents?

The chapters do not follow the same order as the *TARGET* series. They have been shuffled around to give some degree of date order to the book. That is, the first story (Chapter Two) begins with the topic of 'birth' around the 1900s when the century itself had just been born. Midwife Turpin brought thousands of Hessle Roaders into the world; as did two of her daughters and a grand-daughter. They were all registered midwives. Their work in the community depended in turn upon the expectant mother being prepared by an unofficial folk midwife. There was one in almost every street to help with deliveries. One such local wise woman was Granny Gadie who busily helped young and old alike. She was often called in by a worried neighbour to sit with a dying relative, and then to lay out the corpse. The Hessle Road women, therefore, helped each other at times of birth and bereavement.

The next chapter takes us into the Great War, and obviously remains with the topic of life and death. Skipper Edward Rilatt is one of countless Hull war heroes whose brave maritime deeds kept British shores safe from German invasion. He patriotically served his country in both world wars and became one of the most-decorated skippers in the port. Brave though he was, he had an unpredictable temper and so earned the nickname of 'Mad' Rilatt.

Chapter Four homes in upon Hull's herring girls who joined their Scottish sisters as they travelled around the British fishing ports to turn herring into kippers. They worked hard and lived rough, but enjoyed the freedom from a more restricted life at home. Emphasis is given to the travels of 'Cissie' Ashley who went around the country between 1923 and 1937.

In January 1935, the trawler *Edgar Wallace* (H.262) returned to the Humber after a dangerous Christmas trip off Bear Island. Almost home, she 'turned turtle' on Hessle Sands. Only three of the eighteen crew lived to tell the tale. One of those was the cook, Clarrie Wilcockson, who believed himself "the luckiest man on Fish Dock". After the '*Wallace* do' he lost his sea-nerves, but not his sense of humour and went on to earn the nickname of the 'Dancing Bobber'.

The next chapter stays with the theme of lost trawlers. It is about the *STAND* Action Group's initiation of *Lost Trawlermen's Day*. The case is presented for

*This "DON'T BE SHAVED ON SUNDAYS" print is a curiosity which I would like
to solve. What is known is that it was taken at the Hessle-Road-end of Gillett Street
(nicknamed 'Cut-Throat Alley'). It was not a demonstration against the barber's
shop (left) because Henry Holder and his son are standing in front of the placard
(c.1912).
Courtesy Jack Lennard.*

*Summer-time day-trips by bus were a feature of Hessle Road life. Not much
information is available about this group in Goulton Street (usually called 'on Bank'
– c.1950s); but the outing could have been organised by a social club, church, public-
house, or even a corner shop.
Courtesy Sarah Gray.*

the 26th January being marked as an annual tribute to the unsung Hull trawlermen who gave their lives for the port and country in times of peace and war. Also mentioned is the group's related campaign to save the lockhead and riverside buildings on the old St. Andrew's Fish Dock. These 'sacred' buildings are the last relics of when Hull was 'the greatest deep-sea trawling port in the world'.

Back to the community, and the world of the clog-maker. The title of Chapter Seven is "Cloggie Walsh: Everybody Knew Him..." or thought they did. In fact, there was never a clogger named Walsh in business on Hessle Road. There was, however, a Welshman who happily adopted this trade nickname.

Eddie Reynolds of the Brighton Street Methodist Mission is largely responsible for the next chapter. Originally, he wrote to me (January 1988) because he wished to ensure that his lively church got mentioned in the history books. And quite right too. We have since been in regular contact and I am continually amazed by this dynamic place of worship. The *TARGET* articles (Nos. 7-8) generated masses of interest from former members and I was glad to attend their 1990 Re-union (where I collected more information, of course).

We return to the world of trawling via the motor launch *Kitty* owned by Charles Ayre. He plied the Humber for nearly fifty years until 1973. His river taxi ferried many strange passengers from eccentric compass adjusters to Nazi engineers. The *Kitty* was never far from danger in the vicious Humber. Charles was involved in various forms of risky salvage and war-time work.

The original *Hessle Road Corner* series contained four sets of articles related to the superstitions of the fishing community. Three of these (about Cats, Green, and Friday the Thirteenth) have been omitted from this book (and saved for the next one). But I did want to include the one about 'P-I-G'. "Grunter: Trawling Taboo" outlines how a pre-historic Pagan ritual was still 'practiced' by twentieth-century trawlermen in the form of a strict taboo.

Still with the trawling world, Chapter Eleven describes how the *Mohican* (H.391) was wrecked at Iceland — Hull's last pre-war trawler loss — in April 1939. My main source for this story of survival against the elements came from interviews with Stephen Mahoney — a great man in his quiet way. He related how the *Mohican* ran aground on the black volcanic ash of Iceland's southern coast, and how pony-back farmers helped in the rescue. He also exposed the gross indifference of the trawler firm when the crew returned to Hull, and of his reactive nerves in the aftermath of the shipwreck.

The twelfth chapter was extra special, and a joy, for me to write. The braiders of Hull are an incredible breed of women. The 'network of sisters' seem to possess a deep insight into life which may be a gift linked with their craft. Like their brothers who fought at sea, these women helped the war-effort when they turned their hand to make the camouflage for the forces.

The war theme is central to the next chapter. The *Warwick Deeping* (H.136) was a noble trawler pounded to the bottom of the English Channel by five German destroyers in October 1940. Thanks to the bravery and prayers of Jim Fuller, the twenty-two crewmen miraculously survived and rowed ashore to the Isle of Wight (where part of this Hull trawler is now featured in the

*'Blessing of the Waters' is a common ceremony in Catholic countries around the
Mediterranean. After the Second World War it became an annual event on St.
Andrew's Fish Dock. It was performed by St.Mary & St.Peter's Church whose
Dairycoates parish included the dock. These Anglicans were 'high church' and this print
shows the choir boys with swinging incense-holders, candles, and crucifixes
– an unusual sight on the dock.
Courtesy Annie Dixon.*

*St.Andrew's Fish Dock was the symbolic 'bridge' between the Hessle Road community
and the deep-sea Arctic fishing grounds. Peak landings were always expected during
Holy Week with the Wednesday before Good Friday being the busy Show Day. This
1934 picture was taken on the Thursday of Easter week, and the kits may have been
from what was known as a 'late-lander' trawler.
Courtesy John Taylor.*

Maritime Museum at Bembridge).

Chapter Fourteen, the last, is the biggest one. Not surprisingly, it is about a larger-than-life character — dare-devil Dillinger. Since I wrote the four-part series (Nos. 11-14), so much more material has been gathered about this man. Some of the new tales have been included in the book, but the rest have been saved for future publications. Dillinger was an exceptional man, to say the least. His psychology is amazing: the clown who laughed to hide a tear. His life of laughter ended tragically. When the *Kingston Turquoise* (H.50) sank in 1965, all the crew were saved except for Dillinger and his dog.

Although all these chapters are different, they all bubbled out of the same vibrant Hessle Road fishing community and its deep-sea trawling industry. Where else in the world could such a wonderful set of people intereact? In my mind's eye I sometimes imagine that perhaps Charles Ayre once ferried cook Clarrie Wilcockson out to a trawler in the Humber; or that Midwife Turpin attended the Women's Bright Hour at the Brighton Street Chapel; or that a net-braider became a herring girl after she lost her fiancé aboard a Hull trawler at Iceland; or did Cloggie Walsh once have a pint in Rayner's with Dillinger? Who knows? One can speculate forever. But what is true, is that they all were associated with the most lively community in the world: *Good Old Hessle Road*.

The title of this book did not come without difficulty. My first impulse was to call it *Hessle Road Corner* — as it was in the original *TARGET* series. But the publisher pointed out that my 1987 book, *Hessle Road*, could easily be confused with one called *Hessle Road Corner*. Umpteen problems with referencing and orders could be caused by a computer which reads, say, only the first ten letters of any title. Thinking up another title is not as easy as it sounds. For a long while I used "Heydays of Hessle Road" as a working title, but was never truly happy with it. When I mentioned this problem to my friend John Crimlis he immediately suggested *Good Old Hessle Road*. This struck the right chord, especially as it is from the chorus of Pete Smith's memorable song about the community.

The choice of picture for the book cover was very easy. I have always liked the scene of this Hessle Road D-tram passing St. Barnabas' Church and the Fishermen's Memorial at the corner of the Boulevard. This picture has long been featured on a postcard (No.14) issued by the Local History Archive Unit at the Hull College of Further Education (Park Street). The image re-produced on this book, however, came from Millie Harrison's own postcard. We met at the Hessle Evening Townswomen's Guild where I gave a talk. The members had been invited to bring along material related to the Hessle Road community and she entered this card for the competition. I was asked to judge the items and this one naturally took my eye as the best. She kindly agreed to lend me the card, and so the book cover is based upon her family heirloom.

Finally, this is my fourth book about the same community, and the more I find out about the people, the more I want to find out about them. Each chapter gives only a brief glimpse into the rich life experienced in *Good Old Hessle Road*. As a writer, I am privileged to be able to relate their human story. My only hope is that I can fully convey the Hessle Roaders life to you, the reader.

*Decks awash as the **St.Celestin** (H.192) battles homeward from the White Sea. This powerful picture highlights some of the many dangers faced by the trawlermen. In conditions such as these, many a Hull deckhand was washed over the low ship's rail, never to be seen again. Conversely, there are stories of men being washed overboard by one wave and back on deck again by another!*
Courtesy Stephen Mahoney.

CHAPTER TWO

MIDWIFE TURPIN:
STAND AND DELIVER

Midwives are respected figures, and this was especially so in 'Good Old Hessle Road'. Indeed, many older people still remember the name of the midwife who delivered them; such was the esteem these women had within the homes of the fishing families. Some of the remembered names are Fozard, Harrington, Lister, Randall, Skelton, Stark, Waddingham and Midwife Turpin.

The name Turpin is well-known because three generations of midwives from this family practiced in the community. Between them, they brought thousands of babies into the world. And, so well-loved were these women, that some grateful mums named their daughters after them. Grandma Julia Turpin was a midwife between the 1880s and the mid-1930s. On her front door at 17 Eastbourne Street she had a big brass plate which proudly proclaimed:

MRS. JULIA TURPIN

REGISTERED MIDWIFE

In her navy-blue uniform, Julia was a familiar sight as she rode around on her sit-up-and-beg bicycle which had a basket at the front. In this she carried her big black Gladstone-like bag "with all her works inside" — her instruments for the delivery (forceps, scissors, vials of carbolic, etc.). Before the National Health Service was established (1948), there were very few medically-trained midwives. This meant that the demand for her child-delivery skills was never ending. She was on call every hour of the day, every day of the week, and every week of the year.

By the time she arrived at the house, the mother-to-be had usually been prepared by a neighbour — typically, an older woman who acted as the unofficial (folk) 'midwife' in her street (or terrace). Plenty of water would be on the boil to sterilise instruments and for washing purposes. The bed would be made up with old, but clean sheets, maybe with a rubber sheet underneath (to save the mattress from stains). In some houses, newspapers were used on the bed — not only because it was cheap and plentiful, but also because it was said that the printers ink was antiseptic. An emptied drawer or wash-basket was padded out with pillows as a make-shift cradle ready for the new arrival. In the narrow Hessle Road terraces, passers-by could hear a woman in labour when she screamed out. Not all births went smoothly. Members of the Turpin family recount grim stories of when deliveries went wrong and, even worse, when a death occurred of either the mother, the child, or both. Infant mortality was very high in the years of the 'hungry thirties'.

Julia Turpin, herself, was born in 1868 in a village on the banks of the Ouse and her mother, Hanna Stark, was a folk midwife in the area. Julia grew up there and later married engine-driver George Turpin from nearby Cliffe in the 1880s. He had a very broad Yorkshire accent and his surname originated from the Viking word "Thor-pan" meaning God of War. George was employed by the North Eastern Railway Company and the couple may have moved to Hull soon after their marriage. With both himself and Julia working, they were relatively better-off than most of their neighbours. As an engine-driver, he was able to get fresh eggs and butter cheaply (or free) from the farmers he knew along the track. He was an avid listener to the more serious operas, especially the heavier works of Wagner which he enjoyed on one of the early wind-up gramophones. It is claimed that George had the first wireless in the Hessle Road area: a B.T.H. double-crystal set with Daventry coils. With the aerial hung out of the window, he listened through a pair of ear phones. Julia always knew when her husband was on his way home. George blasted a distinct cock-a-doodle-do on the train whistle as he passed the nearby Dairycoates level-crossing.

The Turpins both worked hard. Julia, of course, was called out in all weathers. One evening she set off to a confinement in the middle of a violent storm when chimney-stacks were blown down and a great deal of damage was done. Julia was hit by a falling tile which broke her arm. Frequently, she got soaked to the skin and, as a result, suffered rheumatism. Various treatments were attempted to relieve the severe pains. At one time she had injections of gold. Another remedy was her electric charger which she used in the living room. First, she placed her feet in warm water with an oven plate on the bottom of the bowl. Next, she held grips in each hand which were attached to a large battery. The voltage could be increased depending on the desired effect and caused a current to shoot down her legs and into her feet. At other times, she attached the apparatus to a special metal comb which sent the shock through her scalp.

In contrast to this harsh physical treatment for her rheumatism, Julia also tried spiritual healing. Indeed, she was a very keen Spiritualist and regularly attended the Eastbourne Street (Dairycoates) Mission. In addition to her Spiritualist activities, Julia attended various "Women's Bright Hour" groups at different churches in the neighbourhood. Her favourite hymn was "The Old Rugged Cross" which she often sang on her rounds.

Grandma Turpin was a strong-minded, educated woman. All around her house were thick medical tomes. She was the 'local wise woman' whom people respected because of her depth of knowledge and seemingly magical skills at a time of family crisis. Some of her descendants remember Julia as "a bit of a dragon who sat in her chair and laid down the law to everyone around". Nevertheless, she was well loved. Even when the Turpin's eight children were married with families of their own, they all returned on Sundays to their parents' Eastbourne Street home for "a game of housey-housey and a good old sing-song around the piano".

Julia Turpin died in 1936 after a life-time dedicated to bringing newborns into the fishing community of Hessle Road. Just as a post-script to her life with babies, there is an eerie tale about her home at No. 17 Eastbourne Street. A young lad who was brought up there, decades after the Turpins left, often

Julia Turpin looks proud in her midwife uniform (c.1900). Even in the 1920s, it is said she was one of only four qualified midwives in the whole of Hull. Julia was a familiar sight in the community – "better known than the postman". With a name like Turpin, as might be expected, there were frequent jokes about 'stand and deliver'.
Courtesy Stan Futty.

Large families in small houses were a feature of Hull's fishing community in the early part of the century. This 1917 Gillett Street print shows a group of children down one of the terraces. The bootless kids reflect the popular image of Hessle Road childhood. But some youngsters went barefoot because they hated to wear boots and could run faster without them. On the back of this print is simply written "Our Gang".
Courtesy Nora Dunning.

Two of Julia Turpin's daughters – Olive and Sylvia – followed her footsteps into midwifery. This is Olive in June 1925 with the Lewis triplets born in Rugby Street (No.2 Fern Villas). The middle child was named Olive Sylvia after the Turpins. Olive Turpin (she married a cousin and kept her surname) lived at No.26 Division Road – in the heart of the fishing community.
Courtesy Stan Futty/Bill Lewis.

This 'mountain of children' gives some indication of the high birth-rate and why midwives were kept so busy in the community. This 1919 outing, organised by the 'Little' Neptune Inn, was probably a day trip to Beverley Westwood or 'With' (Withernsea – an east coast seaside resort). Notice the cheeky lad who clambered up on to the top right parapet of the pub!
Courtesy Sarah Gray.

heard the sound of babies crying within the house. He dismissed the noises at the time and never dared tell anyone about them. It was only when he read the "Midwife Turpin" story in the *TARGET* (4th January 1990) that he got a strange feeling and perhaps an 'explanation' of what the sounds meant.

Julia left behind a family of five girls and three boys. Two of the daughters, Olive and Sylvia, followed in their mother's foot-steps and served as midwives in Hull's fishing community. Indeed, when Julia retired, Olive took over her practice. She married a cousin, an engine-driver like her father, and so continued the Turpin name. Also like her mother, she was a keen Spiritualist. Olive delivered around 3600 Hessle Roaders before she retired in 1939. The midwifery torch was carried into the next generation by her daughter who became Mrs. Sylvia Shepherd. Sylvia practiced as a midwife for twenty-four years and delivered over 2000 babies in the neighbourhood. When she retired in 1958 four generations of midwifery, begun by Julia Turpin's mother in the early-Victorian times, were brought to an end.

Another midwife story, from the 1950s, tells of a young (unknown) trainee who was sent to the fishing community. As she prepared an expectant mother for the delivery, the grandmother of the family also hovered around. During their chatter, the older woman told of her work as a fish filleter. The novice midwife casually remarked that it sounded fascinating. The grandmum left the room and the nurse continued to lay out her carefully sterilized instruments on a table by the bed. A few moments later the granny returned with a cod and her old filleting knives. She then happily showed how to carve up a fish on the table with all the clean implements. The mother-in-labour and the midwife looked on amazed as they endeavoured to bring the baby into the world.

Emphasis so far has been given to medically-trained midwives. In Hessle Road, however, practically every street or terrace had its own unofficial folk midwife. They were usually elderly women to whom the younger ones turned during life-and-death crises. Granny Gadie of Wassand Street was one of these wise women who was "always up and down the street helping others". One day she might help bring a child into the world, the next be called in to lay out a neighbour who had just passed away.

A frantic mother from across Granny Gadie's terrace (Crown Place) once dashed over because the doctor had said her two-year old son was beyond help. The grossly under-weight boy had a raging fever (possibly pneumonia). Granny's first remedy was to place him in a mustard bath — to 'fight fire with fire' — which calmed his red-hot temperature. For the next two days she carefully nursed him better. The lad survived and grew up to become a successful Hull businessman.

At times of death, Granny Gadie was called in to sit with an elderly person about to pass away. She was once asked to sit by an old friend of the family down Bean Street in the late 1950s. The old woman was unconscious and the family doctor said she had little time to live. Elizabeth Gadie believed otherwise. She patiently peeled grapes to squeeze the sweet juice onto the lips of her friend. Granny never left the bedside and after a few days her childhood friend recovered and lived for a further three years.

What these and other midwife tales show is the high degree of self-help

The Turpin midwifery lamp was carried into a third generation by Sylvia Shepherd (née Turpin) who also served Hull's fishing families. She retired on 4th June 1958 and is seen here with her mother Olive Turpin. Her retirement party took place at the Domiciliary Midwives Clinic in Coltman Street – from where she was based.
Courtesy Stan Futty.

Wagonette rides along Hessle Road to Pickering ('Picky') Park were a memorable experience for many youngsters. Carting agent Henry 'Sweat' Haines' wagon is loaded with kids outside Paragon Station in 1910 – perhaps on Empire Day.
Courtesy Ron Haines.

which took place within the Hessle Road community. When people recall how 'everybody helped everybody else', they have in mind some of these local wise women who were able to draw upon ancient home-spun remedies to heal others.

Elizabeth Gadie was a folk midwife for the Wassand Street area (she lived down Crown Place). A neighbour recalled how "if any kids in our street had 'owt wrong and the family couldn't afford to have the doctor, they sent for Mrs. Gadie who'd say if it was measles, whooping cough or whatever. She'd tell 'em what to get from Edward Hindle's chemist shop on Hessle Road (No.218) – perhaps a bottle of linctus for 2d.".
Courtesy Alf Louth.

*Skipper Ted 'Mad' Rilatt (left) and the gun crew of H.M.D. **Dawn** who sank a German U-boat in a fierce North Sea fight-to-the-death battle. The tall Newfoundlander lost two fingers in the breech of the gun (which he is standing behind) during the rapid shell fire. The **Dawn** survived the war and was converted to a drifter called the **Expanse**.*
Courtesy Ted Rilatt III.

*The **Pomona** (H.462) was a 'bridge-aft-sider' steam trawler built in 1899 by Cook, Welton & Gemmell of Beverley for the Hull Steam Fishing & Ice Co. (or 'Red Cross' fleet). It was in this ship that skipper Rilatt rescued sailors from two Royal Navy destroyers. This vessel returned to Hull after the war and was transferred to Milford (M.212) in October 1928.*
Courtesy Malcolm Fussey/Christian Ford (Bernard print).

CHAPTER THREE

'MAD' RILATT:
WAR HERO

Hull trawlers and crewmen were at the cutting edge in both world wars (see also Chapter 13). With guts and cunning they carried out the most dangerous naval tasks. Yet they still get little credit for their wartime bravery and the dangerous duties they performed. Our trawlermen swept safe channels through seas alive with deadly explosives; laid mines within the enemies shipping lanes; hounded U-boats with depth-charges; escorted convoys across the Atlantic and north to Russia; guarded river mouths; and, manned boom defence vessels. They were Britain's claws of war which dug deep into the enemy's flesh.

Being at the gory core, they also paid a very high price in life and limb, trauma and trawlers. During the First World War, 135 Hull trawlers were lost. Most of these (73) were civilian losses. On one day alone, 3rd May 1915, seven Hull trawlers were sunk during U-boat attacks. These were the *Bob-White* (H.290), *Coquet* (H.831), *Hector* (H.896), *Hero* (H.886), *Iolanthe* (H.328), *Northward Ho* (H.455), and *Progress* (H.475). They were all sunk by a German U-boat(s) in the same area of the North Sea (approximately 155 miles ENE of Spurn Point, Yorkshire). They were peacefully trawling the Dogger Bank fishing grounds when the Germans took them by surprise.

What tended to happen in this sort of attack was that the trawlermen were forced to surrender or be blown out of the water with their ship. The crewmen were sometimes taken prisoner or, more often, set adrift in a rowing (coggie) boat. The U-boat commander seized the ship's registration documents (like a scalp, it was proof to his superiors that he had sunk the vessel). Next, a time-bomb was placed on board the empty trawler below the water line. Or bullets were fired into the side of the vessel. A torpedo was rarely 'wasted' on a relatively cheap trawler.

There are countless untold stories of what Hull trawlermen endured in the First World War. One tale of valour relates to Edward Spencer Rilatt the Second. This patriotic fighter was to become one of the port's most decorated skippers in both world wars. Like many trawlermen he had a nickname. But his, 'Mad' Rilatt, was none too flattering. He had a fiery temper and it is said that "his head literally used to steam" when he got mad. He even took a certain pride in this name. If someone asked, "What do they call you, then, mate?", his usual reply was, "Rilatt's the name and, if you must know, it's 'Mad' Rilatt!". When annoyed he angrily yanked off his cap, flung it to the floor, jumped on it, and did a little stomping dance. But that was the peak of his ire.

Soon after, it was all over and forgotten. Yet when on the rampage, he was unpredictable. Rilatt once went berserk with a ginger-headed deckhand, Norman Leech, aboard the Hull Northern trawler *Tamora* (H.853). In a blind

German mines were a serious problem in the 1914-18 War and caused enormous losses to British shipping. Thirty-two Hull trawlers were sunk by mines. The Admiralty formed the Mine Clearance Service to counteract this deadly menace. This is the arm badge worn by members of the service.
Courtesy Frank Frankland.

*In March 1926 Ted Rilatt bought a £100 share in the **King Emperor** (H.202) which was owned by Hull fish merchants H. Percival & Sons. Ted is on the bridge verandah and bosun Green of Tyne Street is in front of the winch (c.1928). Cheekily perched outside the bridge is Ted's youngest son Eric (born 1920) on a 'pleasure' trip. Sadly, Eric was later killed on naval duty aboard the Hull trawler **Sedgefly** (ex. **Norman** H.28) mined in the North Sea on 16th December 1939.*
Courtesy Ted Rilatt III.

rage to get to the poor man, he made an enormous leap from the wheelhouse; but mis-judged his landing, struck the winch gear, and broke a leg in two places.

The Germans also felt the wrath of the Rilatt temper when he was skipper of *H.M.D. Dawn*. This was a purpose-built World War One drifter specially adapted as a mine-sweeper (constructed in 1918, and re-named *Expanse* after it was transferred to peace-time fishing). Along with two other British vessels, Rilatt was busy checking the location, to clear a safe channel, when a U-boat suddenly broke surface. The Germans began to shell the armed British ships. A frantic battle ensued as rapid shell-fire was exchanged. The *Dawn's* gunner was a tall Newfoundlander. With Mad Rilatt's daring seamanship and the gunner's accurate shooting, they sank the U-boat despite the odds. During the violent action and quick loading of shells, the big Canadian lost two fingers in the breech of the gun. The whole crew were highly commended for their bravery.

Earlier in the war, Ted Rilatt had been "mentioned in despatches" for an idea which led to the sinking of another U-boat. The Germans and British regularly played a cat-and-mouse game with regard to the laying of mines. The Kaiser's submarines laid a new minefield, next day the British sweepers cleared a safe way through, and the following day the systematic Germans were back to lay more mines. During a strategy meeting with senior officers at Harwich, Mad Rilatt firmly argued a case NOT to sweep a particular field one day. The idea being to "let the Germans get tangled in their own muck". Sure enough, the next day, a U-boat was found washed up on the beach.

Edward Spencer Rilatt, was therefore, a wily character — to both friend and foe. Like many Hull trawlermen, he was his own man who did not take too easily to the Royal Navy's hierarchy and regulations. There is one story which illustrates this well.

Aboard the requisitioned Hull trawler *Pomona* (H.462) Skipper Rilatt, based at Aberdeen, was laying mines between Scotland and Norway. A British destroyer happened to steam nearby when it was hit by a torpedo. Instinctively, Ted went to the rescue. Amongst the survivors taken aboard the *Pomona* were two Liaison Officers from the French Navy. During the course of this operation, a second Royal Navy destroyer came alongside. The captain ordered Rilatt to "get out of the way you confounded trawler!" It seems he wanted the glory of the rescue all to himself. The bedraggled survivors were, therefore, transferred from the 161-ton *Pomona* onto the destroyer. No sooner had the men got aboard the second RN ship when the U-boat "fished him as well". A massive loss of life resulted with bodies everywhere. Various ships were involved in the rescue. The 107-foot *Pomona*, ironically, saved four Frenchmen this time — the two Liaison Officers from the first destroyer and two more from the second.

When Ted landed his survivors, the RN Captain of the second destroyer was on the dockside to greet him. He held out his hand as a gesture of gratitude and respect. Mad Rilatt, however, still furious at what had happened at sea, spat on the captain's hand and walked past him. For insubordination of a superior officer, Mad Rilatt was arrested and placed in detention. But he was released the next day. He never found out why, but guessed that the four French

*Honorary Lieutenant-Commander RNR (Patrol Service) Edward Spencer Rilatt the Second, M.B.E., R.D., Croix de Guerre, was eager to serve his country for the second time in its fight against Germany. The Admiralty gave the patriotic Hull skipper command of the B.D.V. **Barbican** at Swithergate where he guarded a major entrance to Scapa Flow for most of the war years.*
Courtesy Ted Rilatt III.

officers had protested at his arrest, Nevertheless, Edward received no British decoration for his daring rescue work. The French Government intervened to grant him their country's highest honour — the Croix de Guerre with palms (the equivalent of the British Victoria Cross, which some feel he deserved).

Even in the calmness between the wars, danger was drawn to Rilatt like a magnet. In 1925, aboard the *King Emperor* (H.202), he trawled up an unexploded mine. His eldest son, 12-year-old Edward Spencer Rilatt the Third, was on a 'pleasure trip' with his dad during that voyage. Ted Junior recalls how an ugly-looking mine thudded onto the deck of the *King Emperor*. Luckily, its impact-detonation horns were skywards when it came down with a thump. Most of the eleven-man crew dashed to the stern of the trawler to get cover in the galley area. Mad Rilatt, however, leapt atop of the mine and sat with his legs astride it. He ordered young Ted to see the chief engineer, Arthur Walker, to fetch a large hammer and big shifting spanner. After the lad handed the tools up, his dad told him, "Now get aft with them yellow so-and-so's". And added, "If you hear a big bang, tell your mother where I've gone". He then proceeded to remove each of the half-dozen deadly horns and tossed them overboard. The harmless mine was then placed in some old netting, winched up over the side and dumped in the North Sea away from the fishing grounds.

Although Edward was 52 at the outbreak of the Second World War, he "nattered the life out of the Admiralty to let him serve his country yet again". They eventually gave in to his patriotic persistence. He was made Commanding Officer of the Boom Defence Vessel *Barbican* at Swithergate, Scapa Flow from May 1941 and served there for five years. Even this routine guard work was not without Mad Rilatt's colour and sparkle. By the end of his naval service, Edward — in addition to his French honour — had been decorated by the British with two campaign medals from WWI, three from WWII, two long-service medals (including the Royal Decoration), and honoured as a Member of the British Empire. A senior Royal Navy officer certified that Edward Spencer Rilatt had "conducted himself to my entire satisfaction at all times. A most efficient Commanding Officer ... a good disciplinarian [who] displayed continued interest throughout a long period in charge of a main entrance to Scapa".

At the age of 67-years old, Edward was appointed Honorary Lieutenant-Commander, RNR (Patrol Service). He died three years later in September 1957. The packed funeral service was conducted by Pastor Tom Chappell at the Fishermen's Bethel on Hessle Road. And one of the Hull Daily Mail obituaries declared, "Farewell to a Colourful Seafarer".

*Ted and Annie Rilatt at the Cowden caravan camp site (on the east coast near Hornsea) around 1950. Their holiday home was named **Barbican** after the Boom Defense Vessel Ted commanded during most of the Second World War at Scapa Flow.*
Courtesy Laurie Forth.

*Neighbours in Whitfield Avenue (Division Road) at their Peace-Party (November 1918). Practically every terrace in the fishing community put out the flags and did its own Peace-Tea. Most of the people in this print are dressed up. On the sailor's hat (of the girl kneeling on the front row) is written H.M.S. **Victory**.*
Courtesy Mary Welburn.

CHAPTER FOUR

HERRING GIRLS:
ON TENTERHOOKS

Stories of the Scottish herring girls are well-known. Various books and many articles have been written about them. There are many tales of how they travelled around the British fishing ports to preserve the catches of the herring fleets. The Scotsmen who crewed the large fleets of steam drifters were often related to the women who travelled ashore. Margaret Bochel (1982) quotes how the 'fisher lassies' worked very hard "for the love o'oor menfolk. If we hadn't worked, they couldn't have sold their fish" (p33). When these Scottish lassies came on their travels to stay in Hull's fishing community, cheeky young lads shouted after them, "Can you skin a herring, Maggie?" Their rapid response was, "Yes, and I'll skin your arse if I get hold of you!".

Little, however, seems to have been written about the 'Herring Girls of Hull' — their work and adventures. They had all the necessary skills to turn a herring into a kipper and some travelled around the country to work alongside their Scottish sisters. Louisa "Cissie" Ashley of Gillett Street was one of these Hull-born herring girls who travelled to the various fishing ports during the 1920s/30s. Aged fifteen, and just sacked from her first job at Scotter's Jam Factory (caught eating a strawberry), she was at the end of her terrace (Bainton's) when approached by a woman. "Would you like a job tentering herring?" asked Georgina Louth from Inkson's Fish Curers. Cissie said she had no idea how to do it, but was told, "I'll learn you".

Early next morning Cissie was there at the Eastbourne Street smoke-house with Harriet, a friend from her street. They were told to put on a pair of wellies and an oil-skirt (clothes they would have to buy themselves if accepted for the job, as well as white abb boot socks and a 'Scotch turban' head-scarf). The next protective item was vital — 'thumb rags'. Tentering was impossible without these. Mrs. Louth placed a strip of white calico (strong cotton cloth) on the girls' thumbs. This she folded over, wrapped around several times and tied with a piece of string — it could then be slipped off and on when needed. With their thumb rags on, the young girls were shown how to stretch a split herring onto the needle-sharp tenterhooks. They must have done well because both were taken on as herring girls. And they kept their jobs despite being told off by the foreman for bringing too many sweets into work (from Harriet's parents' shop).

The turning of a herring into a kipper involved four main stages. It had to be split, soaked in brine, tentered, and smoked. When Cissie and Harriet had some spare time from tentering, and no-one was about, they were keen to master the first stage of the process — "we learnt ourselves to split herring". The skill was to insert a sharp pointed knife into the top middle part of the herring's back, over the top of the bone (spine). A neat cut was then made up to the head and then back down to the tail. The fish was opened out by its gills and these were cut away. The guts were removed and the bone scraped clean. All the slime and bits were dropped into a 'gut barrel' (which was later carted off to the Hull Fish Meal factory on St. Andrew's Dock). Sometimes, however, part of the herring's guts were saved. These were the two melts and the two raws. The melts were picked out, placed in a bowl, and later sent to London for their oil. The melts could also be washed and eaten as a delicacy by the 'upper crust' (similar to an oyster). Or, as Cissie recalls, after a good night out, "it would take your hang-over off you".

Eventually, despite some of the tricks the new girls got up to, they joined the older women at the herring bench. They had to buy their own herring knife —from Tiplady's of West Dock Avenue, where they had bought their work clothes. The knives were usually sharpened by the men at Inkson's, on a stone, and then with a steel file. A group of about eight or nine women split herring at the long bench. These were happy times for Cissie and she recalls how the women "sang from morning to night". They had a good laugh when they changed the words of popular 1920s songs into their own saucy lyrics. And 'the language they came out with' sometimes shocked even the workmen. The usual working hours were from six-to-six. But at peak landings, if all the herring was not cleared by 6 p.m., they had to work until it was all racked up in the smoke-house.

Once a herring was split, it was dropped into a basket by the side of each woman. Every so often a workman came along to "cobb up". That is, tip each basket into a larger one before the split herring went into the vat of cold brine (a thick salty orange liquid). When the big vat was full, the top layer of herring were neatly arranged and salt scattered over them. The soaking — the 'kipper dip' — took about twenty minutes. Next, the men transferred the soaked fish into 'trows' (tubs) on bogeys ready for the girls to tackle the tentering stage. They were asked, "Whose turn is it to prick on?" — a question which usually got some rude retorts. It was this third stage of the work which made fish-curing a messy job because the girls got covered in brine, their hands, arms and faces were splashed with the orange liquid.

The women worked in pairs at each side of a trow. With their thumb rags on they opened up the herring to prick it, under each gill, onto the tenterhooks. In effect, the herring was stretched between the hooks (the everyday expression "on tenterhooks" means 'being in a state of anxiety' — this suggests that a person's nerves are *stretched* to the limits). The hooks were along a stick or 'boak' placed over the trow so that excess brine dripped back into the tub. Each girl got ten fish on her side of the boak. The one who finished first reached over to help the other complete her side. The full stick was then "run on to the rack" on the other side of the covered yard. The pace of work was very fast indeed, the girls had to dash back and forth. When the rack was full with seven tiers of boaks, it was quickly handed up to another girl who stood on a wall (at the foot of the smoke-house). She in turn handed it up to a man inside the smoke-house. As they handed up the racks, the brine dripped down on them and they were soaked to the skin.

I have very few prints related to the herring girls, especially ones in Hull; but Ron Haines recognised his mother Rose Jane (née Bell – second woman from the right on the front row). She was born in Yarmouth (1881); followed the herring boats along the east coast and travelled as far as Fraserburgh; worked for Pickering & Haldanes (Hull); got married; and lived in Strickland Street. She and three other women are wearing 'Scottish turbans'. One of the lads is Albert Warcup.
Courtesy Ethel Warcup.

Unfortunately, the herring girls were looked down on by outsiders, and some considered their filthy work as 'the lowest of the low'. But the girls themselves were highly satisfied with their job because of the friendship and laughter which grew out of their awful work. Their jokes and songs made the unbrearable bearable. The herring girls once played a trick on the women in the kipper-cutlet section. They gathered some maggots from the floor and spread them over the cutlets. They often expected to get sacked because "we were always giggling and mucking about".

At six in the evening, when the tired girls went home, the smoke-man came on to do his night work. He set the 'mush' (sawdust) alight to smoulder during the night to smoke the herring. If the women worked late and got hungry, they often wrapped herrings in greaseproof to smoulder on the mush: "they were lovely to eat". By six the next morning, the smoke-man had got all the racks of kippers down in the yard ready for the girls to pack. This was a clean job. The girls did not do the same work day-in-day-out, but were on a rota system which gave them some variety. When a 14-lb wooden box was full, the kippers were covered with a sheet of greaseproof, two strips of wood were placed on top and the girls hammered home four nails to secure the lid. Tallies (address labels) were then stuck on the boxes which were sent to fish wholesalers all over Britain.

The kipper work was only seasonal, however. When the herring boats stopped landing, many of the girls were stood-off. Cissie was out of work again, and so went to stand at the top of her terrace to watch the people go by. She was not unemployed for long. A man from Gillett Street suggested she try for a 'travelling job' as a herring girl going to different fishing ports. He sent her to see fish curer Benjamin Tozer at 109 St. George's Road where she was given 2/6d. (12.5p) 'signing on' money, a rail ticket to Scarborough, and two tallies to stick on a travelling box (for her clothes, oil-skirt, boots and knives). Cissie was told to tie up her box with a clothes line and it would go by lorry to the Scarborough fish factory.

When Cissie told her parents "Mother went mad and said, 'You're NOT going travelling!' ". Dad's view was, "She'll never stick it". Although very fond of her mother, she did 'travel' and did 'stick it' for fourteen years (1923-37). She travelled with other Hull girls, mainly from the Gillett/Havelock Street area, called Kitty Elsworthy, Evelyn Jameson, Millie Lee, Ivy Taylor, and Doris Weston — "a real good gang". As well as Scarborough, some of the other fishing ports Cissie and the girls travelled to were, in England: North Shields, Blyth, Yarmouth, Grimsby, and Peel (Isle of Man); and, in Scotland: Fraserburgh, Gourock (near Greenock), Girvan, and Mallaig (both on the west coast). Generally, the girls lodged together at the same digs. If one of them stayed out beyond the landlady's strict 'be-in-by-ten' rule, the others tried to sneak her in by unlocking the front-door or opening a window. At Yarmouth one of the girls crept downstairs with a candle to let her friend in, but the landlady caught her in the act and gave them both hell.

Men and women had to keep in separate parts of the lodgings. Nevertheless, the big advantage of travelling away from home was the freedom from family restrictions. The girls got drunk and stayed out at dances longer then when in

37

Tiplady's is a trader's name deeply engraved into the Hessle Road culture. Many generations of workers on the fish dock, trawlers, and in factories got their working gear (clothes and equipment) from this West Dock Avenue family firm. This 1913 advertisement stresses Bluettes which were a denim-type fisherman's smock. They also made thick fearnought trousers and rubber smocks.
Courtesy Fanny Gray.

Herring girls in Blyth (9th July 1910). Among these women is at least one who travelled there from Hull – Esther Robinson of Eton Street. The women worked in all weathers. In the bitter winter months, some began their working day by plunging both hands into icy water to harden the skin to the cold and stop their fingers splitting.
Courtesy Stanley Young.

Hull. At Fraserburgh, they looked forward to the Monday night dance which cost one shilling (5p). Monday was a day off because in Scotland it was against the men's religion to work on Sundays — so no fishing boats landed the next day.

In the tiny out-of-the-way places, accommodation was primitive in comparison with the digs or the comforts of home life. In Mallaig, for example, the girls stayed in little wooden huts near the pierhead. These rent-free huts usually had nothing but an open fire-place and bunk beds with straw mattresses and pillows. The girls, sometimes six to a hut, often had to take basic items such as cutlery, pots, and mirrors. Sometimes there was not even a table with chairs, so they used their travel boxes (called kists in Scotland). An empty orange box served as a bedside cupboard — a curtain was hung over the front to 'pretty it up'.

Cissie always travelled with her portable, wind-up gramophone and records. The girls looked forward to a Saturday night. If, late evening, the right knock came on the hut door, they knew it was the local Mallaig blokes they had invited. The men would leave the pub at closing time and bring along a big bag of biscuits. The Hull lasses and Scots lads danced until two in the morning. If the right knock was not heard, no-one was allowed to enter and the late-callers usually went away. One night, when the girls refused to open the door, the lads clambered onto the hut roof and blocked the chimney stack. Smoke soon filled the little hut and forced the girls to let in the gate-crashers.

Every work-day morning, the foreman woke the girls up at 5 o'clock. Each girl took it in turn to set and light the coal fire, make a pot of tea, and butter a slice of bread for the others. Pails of water were carried in from an outdoor tap. A large pan of water was put on the open coal fire to boil. They usually washed their clothes in a barrel of rain water just outside the door of the hut.

The Hull girls were sent from place to place to work wherever the herring boats landed. From Mallaig they sometimes moved on to Girvan. If the boats were late, the women waited on the pier and sang as they knitted jumpers and socks for the winter months. That is, unless the foreman gave them the job of scrubbing clean the sticks and hooks to get rid of clogged up salt and brine. The Hull herring girls worked alongside 'gutter girls' from Scotland and Ireland, whose gutted herring was preserved in barrels with about 800 fish in each. Layer after layer was carefully placed and a handful of salt scattered over it. The women worked as a crew of three: two gutted while the other packed a barrel at a rate of 60-70 herring a minute. The crew filled three barrels every hour. Their hands were red-raw from the salt and, for this backbreaking work, they earned 6d. (2½p) per barrel in 1929. Saturday was payday when Cissie got her 30/- (£1.50) wage — less 1/- stamp for insurance. The Hull girls ran to the local post-office to buy an 8/- (40p) postal order to send home to mum.

Looking back on her hard-working life and travelling days as a herring girl from Hull, Cissie said she enjoyed every minute of it and would do exactly the same if given her time over again. After a pause, she added, "If I was a young girl today, I'd be off to Iceland to work in their fish factories".

*Young 18-year old sailor Clarence 'Clarrie' Wilcockson looks tough and proud in his Royal Navy uniform during the Great War. It was from H.M.S. **Canada** that he volunteered to join an expedition to land on the Belgian coast. His landing-craft struck a mine and there was a high loss of life, but Clarrie was pulled out of the water. This was the first time 'lucky' Clarrie cheated the seas.*
Courtesy Clarrie Wilcockson.

CHAPTER FIVE

EDGAR WALLACE:
ALMOST HOME

"You can't go on the *Edgar Wallace* — I'm begging you!" pleaded Carol Wilcockson who intuitively knew her husband was at risk on his next fishing trip. But Clarrie ignored her warning. Having cheated the sea once before, he firmly believed that *Lucky* was his middle name. As well as this, he liked being a cook with the Newington Steam Trawling Company. They were considered one of the best firms who provided good food for the crewmen. The *Edgar Wallace*, itself, was only nine years old — built in 1925 by Cochrane & Sons at Selby specifically for Newingtons (who named all their vessels after famous authors). At 336 tons, she was a 140-foot coal-burner (Hull registration H.262; Official No. 149042; Port No. 110/1925) with an insured value of £9000.

The skipper was Jim 'Stivey' Stevenson. It was his first trip in charge of the *Wallace* and most of the eighteen crew were also first-timers aboard. Perhaps because it was Christmas week (1934), Newington's runner found it difficult to man the ship: "nobody knew anybody else at the start of the trip", recalled Clarrie. He, being the cook, played a central role in keeping the hard-working crew happy: "when you get cooking for eighteen hungry men, you certainly get cooking!" This was especially so when preparing Christmas dinner. Clarrie said, "I was up all the night baking my pastries". The men were served with the usual turkey, followed by Christmas Duff (pudding). Apart from the meal, the men toiled away as if it was any other day on the fishing grounds. For some reason, Clarrie had spent every Christmas away from home since he left the Royal Navy after World War One.

The three-week Christmas trip off Bear Island provided some good catches and the fish rooms were full when 'Stivey' decided to head for home. The *Edgar Wallace* returned from the perilous Arctic Circle in good time, but then had to wait three days at the mouth of the Humber. Thick fog meant they had to anchor off Spurn Point before they could safely enter the estuary. The fog eventually lifted in the late afternoon (4 pm — 9th January 1935) as darkness fell. The *Wallace* sped upstream on a swift spring tide, and was manoeuvred to swing around just to the west of St. Andrew's Fish Dock. This was not easy because the river was crowded — Clarrie had counted at least thirteen other ships' lights in the area that evening.

As the trawler turned, her bow ran into a sandbank. This was no cause for alarm. The engines were kept going ahead in the hope she would clear. The skipper "did everything according to the rule book". When she did clear, however, the *Edgar Wallace* was precariously broadside to the cruelly quick current. She was swept along helplessly.

A frantic S.O.S. was blasted on the ship's whistle which immediately alerted

41

nearby vessels and people ashore. Many fish-dock workers remember that bitter afternoon and describe how they ran to the Humber to see what was going on. Nothing could be done in the extreme wintery conditions. She struck the Hessle Sands and heeled over to port "like a shot". At that moment, Clarrie was below packing his sea-bag and looking forward to his postponed Christmas with his family in Harrow Street (Olive Grove). Instinctively, Clarrie dropped his gear and scrambled out as best he could. When he got on deck above the galley he unlashed a lifebelt from the ship's rail. After he put this around his waist, he calmly did something which, in the long run, saved his life. The cook put his arm through one of the belt's rope loops, reached for the next one and placed a turn firmly around his left wrist.

Most of the crew had got on the whaleback (over the bow) to get above the rapidly rising water. Clarrie had no time to join them, so he clambered up the mizzen rigging with two others. All around men called out for help. Before too long, however, most were swept from the trawler by the ferocious tide. Skipper Stevenson, mate Gibbons, and chief engineer Maloney were washed off the fo'c'sle together and disappeared into the darkness.

Asked if there was any panic, Clarrie replied, "Trawlermen are not the type to get excited in danger — they are *always* in danger. They take life as it comes". He then quoted an old saying: "Come day, go day" — meaning they did not live for tomorrow, just for today. Added to this, there is a superstition that they need never learn to swim. If the sea gods want you, they get you — so why struggle and prolong the agony. Stories abound in the trawling world of men washed off deck by one wave and washed back by another. Incidents like this showed that their 'time had not yet come', the sea did not want them and so their lives were spared. These beliefs taught the men not to resist the might of nature, but passively accept their fate when it came.

Clarrie was unable to grip the mizzen mast for very long. His hands froze solid, he was forced to let go and was washed along in the torrent. In the bitterly freezing water he was so cold that he could not feel it — his whole body was numb. Unlike most trawlermen, Clarrie was a good swimmer. But he reasoned: "this is a hell of a strong tide, I'm in the middle of the Humber, so save energy and don't try to swim ashore — go with the flow". With his body frozen and his mind resolved, many past thoughts swirled through Clarrie's head. One memory which flooded back was of the last time he was forced to abandon ship. This was when he was an eighteen-year-old sailor in 1918 during the First World War.

In the latter part of the war he served aboard the dreadnought *H.M.S. Canada*. She was armed with thirty guns (including ten 14"), had a 28000-ton displacement weight, and a complement of 1176 men. While aboard this 'big gunner', Clarrie was one of many eager young sailors who volunteered for a 'landing do' (expedition) on the Belgian coast near Zeebrugge. As the fifty landing craft headed ashore, Clarrie's hit a mine. The captain immediately ordered, "Discharge all your heavy weight" — hand-grenades, rifle, and ammunition. Dead bodies floated all around, but Clarrie was one of the lucky ones who was rescued.

He felt himself very fortunate to have survived the Great War. Once

*Clarrie the cook is seen here (on far right) in June 1934 with several trawlermen aboard the **St. Merryn** (H.40) fishing off Iceland. Some of the other men are George Wainburg, Alfred Elsworthy, Bill O'Pray (17-year old deckie-learner), George Taylor, Gus Farrow, and Arthur Sowter.*
Courtesy Clarrie Wilcockson.

*The H.262 Hull fishing registration number of the **Edgar Wallace** can be seen just above the water level in the Humber. The motor launch **Kitty** (see Chapter 9) ferried engineers out to the wreck. In the calm after the storm, salvage engineers from Grimsby fix hazard-warning lights on the mizzen. Clarrie had clambered up this mast during his 'lucky' escape from the doomed trawler. Not so lucky was the **Boatman** tug engineer who drowned during the unsuccessful salvage work on the wreck.*
Courtesy Stephen Mahoney.

demobbed, Clarrie looked for a seafaring job down on St. Andrew's Dock. He considered himself 'lucky' in that he just wandered down on dock and a runner asked, "Are you looking for a ship?". There was a severe shortage of men after the war, so Clarrie became a trawlerman and, later, a cook. Although 'black-balled' by the Hull trawler owners (for 'spragging' to the local Board of Trade — "the biggest crime on dock") and forced to sail out of Grimsby for a spell, he eventually came back to his home port. His 'luck' stuck with him when he decided to quit the *James Long* (H.141) in 1933.

After twelve months of poor catches, the mate said, "Clarrie, I've had enough of landing in debt — I'm chucking it in" and so, as cook, he did the same. Sadly, the thirteen who next sailed on the *James Long* in January that year were all mysteriously lost on her return voyage from Iceland. This incident strengthened Clarrie's belief that "I'm the luckiest man on dock". But would "luck" save him from the merciless Humber which had claimed fifteen of his shipmates from the *Edgar Wallace*? It did.

Blue with cold, after almost ninety minutes in the freezing water, Clarrie caught sight of a ship's lights. With all the might he was able to muster, he shouted as loud as he could. It was the *s.s. Goole*, a coaster based at Goole, which had joined the search for survivors in response to the S.O.S. calls. The crew were on the lookout and heard Clarrie's cry for help. The night was inky black and the seamen could not see Clarrie. They yelled out, "Keep shouting, keep shouting — we can't see you — keep shouting!" The coaster circled three times as Clarrie shouted for all his life was worth. Then he heard a voice carry over the water, "Alright skipper, we've found him".

The Goole men lowered a boat and found Clarrie "almost going under" with his chin barely on the lifebelt. Had he not put that extra turn of the rope around his wrist, he could have gone under. When his rescuers dragged him out of the water, all they heard him repeatedly mumble was, "Thank God. Thank God". With Clarrie safely aboard, the coaster headed full steam to Goole where an ambulance was ready at the dockside.

The next day, in Bartholomew's Hospital, Carol Wilcockson came to see her husband. She stood at the foot of his bed, put her hands firmly on her hips, looked straight at him and simply said, "Well?" Clarence apologised for not taking heed of her sixth-sense about the *Wallace* and promised to listen to her next time. During their re-union, Carol kept secret the painful news that fifteen of his fellow crewmen had been lost in the Humber. It was a week later when he returned to their terraced home that he was shown the Hull newspapers and found out how many had died: "I felt awful — because I was still alive".

Clarrie attended the Memorial Service for the crew of the *Edgar Wallace* at the Fishermen's Bethel on Hessle Road. But he was too distressed to remember anything about it. What did stick in his mind, and cut him deeply, was a skit made by a mother who lost her young son. She remarked, "I see *you* managed to save *your* life then" — that hurt Clarrie. For months he did not sleep because he "was thinking about the good men who'd gone, especially the new skipper who'd not completed his first trip".

Clarrie's next torturous ordeal came at the Board of Trade Inquiry into the Humber tragedy. He was angered by allegations that the skipper was drunk at

44

Dance enthusiasts Carol ('Cal') and Clarrie Wilcockson at a York competition around 1950. His workmates on the fish dock knew he loved to dance and so nicknamed Clarrie "The Dancing Bobber". He eventually lost this job because his nights out meant he was often late to start work at two o'clock in the morning. Courtesy Clarrie Wilcockson.

the time of the loss. Clarrie was very fond of Jim Stivey. He had watched him make his way up from deckie-learner to skipper. The main reason Clarrie had gone on that voyage — leaving his family over Christmas and disregarding his wife's premonition — was because of a bond of loyalty between the two men. The *Wallace* was Stivey's first command and, as he got a crew together, he particularly wanted Clarrie as the ship's cook. So when Clarrie was asked at the official inquiry, "Had the skipper been drinking?", his irritated, but firm answer was, "Yes! A mug of *TEA* I'd taken to him on the bridge".

Clarrie did attempt to go back trawling, but he could not stick it for long. The work was no problem, but he suffered violent nightmares which kept him awake. He heard the men's voices as they called for help and their faces flashed before his eyes. Added to this, the sly innuendoes continued, implying that he survived at the expense of others. Under this pressure, his sea nerves shattered.

The 'Wallace Do' became too much — "I was always on the jump" — so he left the industry for good. With no compensation to speak of, Clarrie was forced to get a job ashore to support his family. He became a bobber for a while landing fish on dock. It was not long before his work-mates affectionately nicknamed him 'The Dancing Bobber' because Clarrie and his wife won many trophies for old-time dancing. But "his dancing came before his bobbing". Consequently, his late-night enjoyment clashed with his early-morning work (2 a.m. start). He was absent and late too often and eventually had to leave the dock. Added to this, his doctor said the wet, cold conditions were bad for his health. So he was out of work again.

Clarrie believed he 'landed on his feet' when he got a job with the Hull Corporation Cleansing Department as a road sweep. He was happy in his work and reluctant to retire in 1965. His boss must have known this and asked if he wanted to become a night watchman at the Chapman Street Depot. He gladly did this until he was eighty-years old. Clarrie was well-liked and given a good retirement send-off.

In his latter years, happy-go-lucky Clarrie had a brief stay in the Hull Royal Infirmary where a strange irony occurred. For the first time in nearly fifty years, his path crossed with one of the other two survivors of the *Edgar Wallace*. A young nurse came over to his bed to ask if he had survived the tragedy in 1935. She then told him that across the way was Charles Hendrick — a former spare-hand from Wellsted Street. Given this chance meeting the two elderly men had a long yarn about what had happened in their lives and of their fortunate escape from the *Edgar Wallace*. No doubt Clarrie laughingly told Charlie, "I've had a happy life and always been very lucky".

CHAPTER SIX

STAND:
LOST TRAWLERMEN'S DAY

There is a time and a place for everything — or so we are told. An exception, however, seems to be the Hull fishing families who grieve for their loved ones lost at sea. This chapter argues for a special time and place when and where relatives can pay their respects to the trawlermen who never returned home from the cruel seas. A case is put for 26th January being declared a *Lost Trawlermen's Day*; and for the construction of a secluded *Garden of Remembrance* at the St. Andrew's Fish Dock Heritage Park.

January 26th is a date drenched in death for the present generation of Hull fishing families. It is one of a handful of specific dates when many Hull trawlers were lost — with a high cost in human life and anguish. Many Hull readers will know the names *Lorella* and *Roderigo* lost on this date in 1955, and the *Kingston Peridot* in 1968. These are just three of eight Hull trawlers lost on 26th January over recent decades.

Not that this is the only black date in the history of Hessle Road suffering. Historically, the worst-ever single-day disaster struck the port on 6th March, 1883 when twenty-four wooden smacks were pounded to pieces in a violent North Sea hurricane. The names of these vessels, in alphabetical order, are: *Andrew Marvel* (H.1092), *Ann Sins* (H.615), *Bernice* (H.1052), *Bessie Lewis* (H. 1170), *Brilliant* (H.896), *Britannia* (H.686), *Burton Stather* (H.247), *Clara* (H.566), *Dove* (H.1033), *Friend's Good Will* (H.711), *Harrier* (H.706), *John Harker* (H.1070), *John Rogers* (H.80), *Lily* (H.904), *Lively* (H.655), *Lizzie Gale* (H.114), *Loch Long* (H.1281), *Mary Esther* (H.1189), *North Sea* (H.926), *Prudence Ann* (H.775), *Sunbeam* (H.632), *The Boys* (H.1084), *Vanguard* (H.1117) and *Water Lily* (H.1197). The *Dart* (H.1062), *Vicuna* (H.?) and *Inflexible* (H.1009) sank within the following two days. It is not too difficult to produce this list of trawler losses for 1883. But it must be remembered that beyond this list are 129 Hull crewmen (and boys) who perished. They left behind sixty widows and around 200 fatherless children.

The blackest month is, of course, December. Many a Hessle Road Christmas has been devastated by the heart-breaking news of trawler losses. Take, for example, 22nd December, between 1884 and 1939 there were thirteen losses on that one day. The first of these was the *Ruby* (H.1032). Then in 1894, nine more were lost on that date: *City of Birmingham* (H.162), *Economy* (H.221), *Energy* (H.218), *Excel* (H.1187), *Express* (H.237), *John Sims* (H.1110), *Londesborough* (H.268), *Sportsman* (H.761) and *Vigilant* (H.1286). The final three were *Moonlight* (H.? in 1897), *Lycurgus* (H.93 in 1908) and *Dromio* (H.94 in 1939).

And on Christmas Day itself there have been nine Hull losses (1858-1973). These were, in date order, the *Yorkshire Lass* (1858), *Sea Flower* (1862),

The dock basin, lockhead and riverside buildings are the ones which STAND wished to have saved, restored and transformed into the St.Andrew's Fish Dock Heritage Park. This wonderful cluster of buildings are the last physical relics of when Hull was "the Greatest Deep-sea Trawling Port in the World". They must be kept not only for the heritage of the port and local families, but also as a magnet to draw tourists to our maritime city.
Copyright Alec Gill.

There is unlimited potential for this historic site which could reflect its former fishing tradition. There is strong support for the idea to dredge out the dock basin and re-introduce fish-related work. The Humber has many small fishing boats (cobles, shrimpers) which need quay space; and there is a mini-industry in the repair of old wooden Danish (snibby) fishing vessels which need workshop space. Alongside these and other enterprises could develop a small flotilla of museum trawlers.
Copyright Alec Gill.

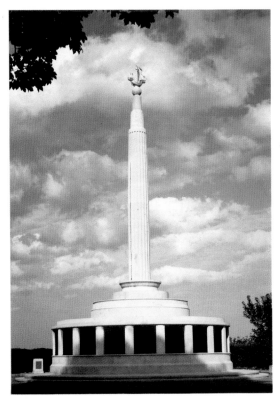

*The Memorial in Lowestoft to the 2385 men who lost their lives in the Royal Navy Patrol Service. Every year, Hull families travel down simply to read the names of their relative killed in the Second World War – names are inscribed on the base of this monument. But why are the hundreds of gallant Hull trawlermen not honoured in their home port? Central to the STAND campaign is the plea for the St. Andrew's Dock site to contain a secluded **Garden of Remembrance** to the **Lost Trawlermen of Hull** – those who gave their lives for others in peace and war.*
Copyright Alec Gill.

The John Crimlis model of the envisaged St.Andrew's Fish Dock Heritage Park is a focal point of the STAND campaign. It was unveiled at the Public Meeting from which the action group was formed (25th September 1989). This is not a definitive model of how the park must be. It was constructed to stimulate debate about whether gardens or water should be in the dock basin. It has been on public display all over Hull in schools, supermarkets, churches, colleges and wherever the STAND committee members collected signatures for their petition.
Copyright Alec Gill.

Elizabeth (H.949 — 1891), *Teutonic* (H.117 — 1906), *Ladysmith* (H.726 — 1911), *Kingston Beryl* (H.499 — 1943), *St. Amandus* (H.247 — 1947), *St. Finbarr* (H.308 — 1966) and *Ian Fleming* (H.396 — 1973).

The significance of 26th January for Hull trawler losses, however, is that there has been a disturbingly high concentration on that particular date since the Second World War. In 1955 the *Lorella* (H.455) and *Roderigo* (H.135) went down after being iced up in the worst-ever recorded sub-zero blizzard 90-miles NE of the Horn of Iceland. With each trawler having a twenty-man crew, the fearsome death toll reached forty.

Exactly thirteen years to the day (after 1955) came the awful loss of the *Kingston Peridot* (H.591). This was the second trawler in the triple losses of 1968 with the disappearance earlier of the *St. Romanus* (H.223 — 11th January) and afterwards the *Ross Cleveland* (H.61 — 4th February). In all, 58 men died (but not on the same date). This dreadful date recurred again in 1984 with the loss of the Hull-based stern trawler *Navena* (FD.323) which managed to beach in Scarborough harbour. Fortunately, her twelve-man crew were safely rescued.

Just as a matter of historical interest, there were four other Hull trawlers which disappeared on 26th January prior to WWII — making an overall total of eight losses. The two earliest ones were the sailing trawlers *Annie* (in 1867) and *Uno* (H.587 — 1883). After the turn of the century, two pre-WWI steam-trawler losses were *Orkney* (H.386 — 1902) and *Gothic* (H.67 — 1910). There were no losses on this January date either between or during the two world wars.

These eight ships represent just under one percent of the nine hundred losses catalogued in *Lost Trawlers of Hull 1835-1987*. I have yet to establish how many human lives have been lost in the Hull trawling industry. Even a guess at 5000 dead trawlermen would be a gross underestimate. The Holland-Martin Inquiry, into the 1968 tragedies, stressed that the majority of fishermen's deaths at sea each year came not with the loss of a trawler, but "the most common cause of death was by losses overboard" (p.13). A higher estimate, but perhaps a more realistic one, could double the earlier figure to around 10,000 Hull crewmen who have died at sea since the Hull trawling industry began (in the mid-1800s). A shuddering figure and thought! A thought, indeed, that leads one to ask: "Where, when and how are these brave trawlermen honoured in our proud maritime city?" Most of these Hull men have no graves; no place of rest but beneath the wild waves. Some families find it hard to accept the loss of their loved one because there is no body, no funeral, and no gravestone to visit.

In a postscript to *Lost Trawlers of Hull* I argued for a befitting memorial to the countless lost trawlermen from the port. The current STAND campaign (1990) for the St. Andrew's Fish Dock Heritage Park intends to incorporate a secluded *Garden of Remembrance* as a tribute to the Hull trawlermen who gave their lives in peace and war for the prosperity of the port and the security of the state. There is widespread support for this form of tribute. Similarly, as well as a *place* to honour our trawlermen, should there not also be a *time*, a special day on which to remember them too? The suggestion is made that this special day be marked each year on 26th January. A time to reflect on what the trawlermen have given for the city of Kingston upon Hull.

After the loss of a Hull trawler there was usually a special Memorial Service for the lost men at the Fishermen's Bethel (and post-1967 at the Royal National Mission to Deep-Sea Fishermen). Although these gave immediate comfort, many relatives were still left with endless doubts. At their time of distress, some women turned to the Spiritualists for an answer. They went hoping for a 'message' to confirm that their husband or son was actually dead. There were many mediums in the Hessle Road area (upto the late-1950s), but two of those most often mentioned are Reg Horton of St. George's Road, and Mrs. Hudson of Regent Street.

Much of the widow's mental anguish arose because there is no grave for her or the family to visit. Our society fails to give them a time or place when they can fully grieve in an acceptable manner. Our culture does not possess an adequate social ritual for the bereaved to fully come to terms with their loss. The cold British 'stiff-upper-lip' attitude is such that it wants to see such emotional matters swept under the carpet. The past and the dead are best forgotten, it seems. Whereas, in some so-called primitive societies, they have long-established set rituals and places where people can vent their grief in a socially-accepted manner. As a nation, we do this every year on Remembrance Day (11th November) ceremonies at Cenotaphs throughout the land. So why not locally for our *Lost Trawlermen of Hull?*

The proposed *Garden of Remembrance* would be *exclusively* for trawlermen and not incorporate other Hull seafarers. The 'big boat' Merchant seamen, deserve their own tribute located somewhere along the East Hull river front. The St. Andrew's Gardens would be a quiet place where relatives and friends could visit on, say, the anniversary of the loss, birthdays, or Christmas. Here, flowers could be placed in a vase and names read on plaques (as is the case with war memorials).

I know of various fishing families who have travelled to visit London's Tower Hill Memorial, or Lowestoft's Royal Navy Patrol Service Memorial just to read their father's or son's name inscribed on a plaque. This gave them a great deal of inner comfort and mental peace — even decades after the loss — to know that their relative has not been completely forgotten.

But why should these Hull families have to trek hundreds of miles? Why is there no befitting place in Hull itself — the men's home port — where people can go to pay their respects and be comforted?

Likewise with a *Lost Trawlermen's Day*, the Churches, Chapels, or Royal National Mission to Deep-Sea Fishermen could hold a special annual service. At this, relatives could place the names of their loved ones on the altar. Prayers could be dedicated to their memory. A special Eucharist could be held or whatever.

The *STAND* Action Group initiated this event on 28th January 1990 (the nearest Sunday to the 26th). The ceremony was held at the St. Andrew's Fish Dock lockhead. It was led by Reverend Derek Smith — vicar of St. John's Newington Church — in whose parish the dock is situated. We were unsure how to set about it, but decided it was best kept simple, not to specifically invite anyone, but to obtain as much media publicity as possible to see who wished to

51

The John Crimlis STAND model has attracted a great deal of public interest in the first year of the campaign to save the old fish dock buildings. The 14,000-plus petition has been gathered at many events and locations: The Fishermen's 1904 Memorial Statue on Hessle Road; firework display and Regatta at the Hull Marina; Christmas shoppers along Whitefriargate; Newland Homes Whit Carnival and, as in the above photograph, at the Hull City Hall CVS Community Fair (with members John Crimlis, Arthur Cowan, Michael Evans and Clive Margerison – February 1990).
Copyright Alec Gill.

*The first-ever **Lost Trawlermen's Day** was held at mid-day 28th January 1990 (the nearest Sunday to the 26th) at the bullnose on St.Andrew's Fish Dock. It was led by the Reverend Derek Smith, vicar of St.John's Newington Church – in whose parish the dock is situated. Around 200 people attended the short ceremony in which an anchor-shaped wreath was blessed, prayers were offered and the hymn **Eternal Father** was sung.*
Copyright Alec Gill.

attend out of their own choice. Even had there been only a dozen *STAND* committee members in attendance, we would have felt the occasion was worth being held.

As it was, we were amazed when around two hundred people joined us at the lockhead service. Reverend Smith blessed the anchor-shaped wreath, it was then carried over to a bollard, tied with a black ribbon, and prayers were offered. Spontaneously, some women brought their own flowers to cast into the waters of the Humber. A frequent comment was that the event should be held again and perhaps even twice a year. This would enable more elderly people to attend in a warmer season (although the day was one of brilliant sunshine, it was bitingly cold). Overall, it was a moving occasion. Some wept. Strangers shared memories. Long-buried grief was released and guilt eased. Towards the end, a small group of us sang (at the request of the film crew) the hymn *Eternal Father*.

We at *STAND* therefore believe that Hull should have a special time and place to remember its lost trawlermen. The time would be 26th January and the place can only be on the site of the former St. Andrew's Fish Dock — from where the men sailed and never returned home.

Fish dock bobbers were the largest workforce to wear the heavy boot-like Hull clogs. Their clogs could usually be distinguished from those of other workers because the thick wooden soles were kept bleach white when they trod about in the ice, especially the 'below men' who worked in the hold of a trawler and freed the wet fish from the ice. This is Charles 'Fred' Gray the Third of Harrow Street at the end of a working day in 1947 on St.Andrew's Fish Dock.
Courtesy Tricia Gray.

CHAPTER SEVEN

CLOGGIE WALSH:
"EVERYBODY KNEW HIM..."

... or did they?" Walsh's Old Clog Shop in Dairycoates was renowned on Hessle Road with its big clog hung over the front of the shop. But was there ever a clog-maker called Walsh who worked in Hull's fishing community? The answer is "No". But this mystery will be investigated after a look at the distinct world of clog-making in the port.

Clogs were worn in many different local industries, but especially by the fish-dock workers. Bobbers in clogs were a colourful part of life in the community. The men began to land the Arctic trawlers at two o'clock in the morning. In the dead of night as people slumbered, the click of their clog-irons echoed around the dockside streets as the men tramped into work. With fond memories people recall, "You could set your clocks by 'em as they marched beneath your window". Clogs were ideal for the bobbers. They kept their feet dry and gave a firm footing as they trod about on slippery ice and slimy fish. An old-time expression was that the fish-dock workers "wanted *warm understandings*, and there's nowt to beat clogs". Their official trade name was a 'high-topped double-tongued clog'. The Hull clog looked more like a large boot than the better-known Dutch or Lancashire clog.

Cloggie Walsh used the best kip leather for the uppers which were fastened onto a thick hardwood (platform-like) sole — especially bought from Snaith, Yorkshire. The tough uppers were fastened to the sole by a welt — a narrow strip of brass, copper, or tin. Nails were carefully hammered through the metal and leather into the wood. The underneath part of the sole was sometimes protected by a sheet of iron. This stopped the wood being hollowed out as the men crunched about on the ice. Clog-irons came next. These horse-shoe-like strips were firmly nailed around the underneath edge of the sole. The toe was capped by a thin piece of metal — the bobbers often kicked anything they wanted to budge.

Some customers watched their clogs being made. A good pair could last years if re-clogged and re-ironed. Heavy usage soon wore the irons down. The clog-makers had to repeatedly tell some young dock workers, "Don't wear 'em down so much. It takes us three times as long to build 'em back up again".

Olive Fisher, who served in Cloggie Walsh's, recalls how slimy and smelly the clogs were when the dock workers came to get them re-done — "not very pleasant, but you soon got used to it". If the workshop men were busy, she used to knock off the old clog irons to speed up the job. Initially, Olive came as a housekeeper to the widowed clog-shop owner (in 1943); but he soon got her to serve in the shop. She did not mind. It was 'company' and got her out of the lonely house off Anlaby High Road. "You bring us luck", he told her, "and the customers like to talk to you" — as they waited for their clogs. Bobbers and merchants often gave fish to the clog-makers by way of thanks for their comfortable footwear. Occasionally, a 'hard up' crewman sold his 'fry of fish' to them, and Olive sometimes passed it on to her friends.

The fishing industry workers were not the only customers of Cloggie Walsh. Different types of lighter clogs were made for various industries throughout Hull. A list from the 1940s includes starch, oil, blue, breweries (extra large clogs for them), dyes, paint, tin works (Metal Box, Gipsyville), the Dairycoates railway depot, and gardeners on their allotments "to keep their feet dry on the wet ground". Clogs were healthy for the wearer. Even some skippers, who paced up and down the trawler bridge for hours on end, wore them to avoid swollen feet. Women also used Walsh's. They went more for the nimble shoe-clog, or knee clog with tops like wellingtons — and some asked for red, blue, or green colours: "the ladies liked colours, a bit smarter, you see".

Before Dorothy Pearson (née Butler) was married, she wore clogs at Binnington's Pickle Factory, Star Works, Regent Street. In her job she used to get wet through and clogs kept her feet dry, at least; but she had to wear men's woollen socks to stop her ankles being chafed. Her clogs were sometimes a problem in winter. When she left work in the snow, it steadily compacted within the clog-irons. She gradually got taller and taller. "By the time I got home, it was like walking on stilts".

Over the years, the shop did one-off orders for dancing clogs, pattens, and tiny fancy clogs for special occasions. And, as a present for some friends, Cloggie Walsh gave them a tiny pair of clogs on their wedding day.

Another Cloggie Walsh story, from 1934, relates to school children. The large Thurston family of Gillett Street (Filey Parade) had to struggle in those years of the Depression on husband William's low wage as a casual bobber. Harietta found it hard to keep her eleven surviving children (three had died young) clothed and shod, especially the boys. Two of them were at Scarborough Street School (aged 6 and 7 years old) and soon wore out their boots. In desperation, Harietta took Tom and Ernest around to Cloggie Walsh to get them measured for a pair of clogs with eye holes which buttoned down the side. The next day the brothers marched into school, clog-irons and all, and sent a clatter along the corridors and around the class-room. Their teacher could not stand the noise and she sent them home to change their footwear. Their mother, sleeves rolled up, stormed into school with her boys. The teacher got an earful as the irate mother told how she could not afford to keep them in expensive boots which soon wore out. The poor teacher backed down and agreed to make an exception. The Thurston lads were allowed to wear their clogs in school. No doubt she lived to regret her decision. Over the next few weeks, more and more pupils turned up at school — their feet clad in the noisy clogs.

Olive remembers opening the shop at seven one morning, and within the first hour she had sold six pairs of clogs. The shop was also a 'grindery' which sold sprigs, hob-nails, leather or rubber soles and heels (for customers who did their own shoe-repairs on a last at home), shoe polish, dubbing, and boot laces (Walsh's cut their own leather laces — when there was a slack moment, that is).

Cloggie Walsh provided new clogs with leather laces – cut individually when his workshop men had the spare time. This clog belongs to ex-bobber John Crimlis who did not like leather laces because they snapped without warning. He and other bobbers replaced them with a piece of twine which clearly showed signs of wearing thin and cost nothing.
Copyright Alec Gill.

Abel Griffiths' first clog shop in the fishing community was at No.39 West Dock Avenue. Abel (left) is with assistant Fred Clare and adopted son Jack Dickinson (right) – each proudly displays their handiwork. This shop was only a short-lived, initial venture into the fishing community in 1926 and should not be confused with the long-established Cloggie Brown family at No.34 West Dock Avenue, who were there between 1908 and the Second World War.
Courtesy Olive Fisher.

57

WALSH'S, FAMOUS CLOG MAKERS

(Late North Bridge)

**Garden and Laundry Pattens. Clogs.
Speciality — FISH DOCK CLOGS.
Only Practical Men Employed.**

531, HESSLE ROAD. Phone 239y5

This 1933 Cloggie Walsh advertisement indicates that Abel Griffiths used the well-established trade name before it appeared in the 1936 Trade Directory. The mention of "Late North Bridge" is evidence of his recent move to the Hessle Road premises in 1930. The phrase "Only Practical Men Employed" means that the clogs were not bought-in, but made entirely on the premises in that the leather was cut out, soles shaped to the individual, and welts fitted.
Courtesy Chris Ketchell.

This is Cloggie Brown's shop at No.34 West Dock Avenue – an old Hessle Road family business begun by Tom in 1908 (until he died in 1943). This is his wife Josephine (née Graysmark) who was born in Brighton (1868) – her parents were boot-makers to Queen Victoria. Her son Leo opened a clog-shop in 1949 at No.527 Hessle Road – only two doors from where Cloggie Walsh had been at No.531 (until 1946 when they moved across the road to No.578). With the premises of Cloggie Brown and Cloggie Walsh being so close at different times over the decades, it is no wonder that they are sometimes mistaken for each other.
Courtesy Leo Brown.

But was there ever a man called *Cloggie Walsh* on Hessle Road? To answer this it is necessary to dig back into history. The main research source used was the Trade Directories at Hull's Local History Library. These show that the original shop was started in East Hull by a James Walsh around 1855 in Lime Street (near North Bridge, Witham). He apparently died about thirty years later and his wife, Margaret, kept the business going for a while afterwards. A Thomas Airey then came on the scene in 1892 at No.4 Lime Street. The name of "Walsh" then disappeared from the Trade Directories, but may have persisted at the local level. Airey traded under his own name until the mid-1920s when he retired to live with his daughter in Canada.

The next clog-maker to take over the "Walsh" business was Abel Griffiths (c.1925). Prior to this, Olive Fisher described how, as a young lad in 1896, Abel made clogs for Welsh coal-miners in Wrexham. Around 1904 he moved to Hull as a 'seatsman' for Thomas Airey at Lime Street. The Welshman worked hard to come up to the high standard set by his new master who was difficult to please.

Before the First World War (c.1910) Abel moved over to Grimsby where he opened up his own "Practical Clog-maker and Fisherman's Outfitter" shop. While over there, he got married to Agnes Broad and they adopted a lad called Jack Dickinson. Jack served his apprenticeship under Abel who insisted upon the best workmanship and could not be answered back. The lad worked so hard that his hands bled sometimes as he handled the rough materials. But Abel was a "good-hearted man. If anyone was really poor, he'd say, 'Knock him a shilling off'". Indeed, his profit margins were low and the standard of workmanship very high — "that's why people came to Cloggie Walsh".

Abel did well in Grimsby, but missed his friends in Hull. When, in the mid-1920s, he heard that Thomas Airey was about to retire he bought his old master's business in Lime Street, and his home in Grosvenor Street. The Welshman opened a clog shop in Hull's fishing community at No.39 West Dock Avenue (c.1926 — see photo), but this was only a very brief venture.

Abel had to wait until 1930 before he could leave the tiny Lime Street workshop to open his first place on Hessle Road itself at No.531. Initially, he traded under his own name. It was only in the 1936 Trade Directory that he officially revived the name *Walsh's Old Clog Shop (Proprietor Abel Griffiths)*. A few years later, in an interview on BBC war-time radio, he claimed that, "my old shop has been on the go since 1855" (*The Listener*, 8th October 1942, p.457). Abel enjoyed it when Hessle Roaders called him 'Cloggie Walsh'. He liked a pint and yarn in the pub. He was a good story-teller who "kept you alive with the tales he told". So the man everyone knew as 'Cloggie Walsh' was not really of that name at all.

The myths and memories of Cloggie Walsh are sometimes mixed with those of rival Cloggie Brown. This was a long-established Hessle Road family business of clog-makers whose premises were sometimes confused with those of Cloggie Walsh. Leo Brown was "born to the Hull clog trade" (1910). His Leeds-born father, Thomas (1865), opened a shop in 1908 at No.34 West Dock Avenue and was there until 1936 (the first confusion arises here because Cloggie Walsh was briefly across the road at No.39 in 1926). Cloggie Brown

Jack Dickinson (above), along with Olive Fisher, took over the Cloggie Walsh business after the death of Abel Griffiths in May 1955. Jack was born in Grimsby (1898), his parents died when he was a lad, and the Griffiths adopted him. Jack was a Signalman in France during the First World War. After the Cloggie Walsh shop closed (18th October 1964), Jack took down the giant clog which had hung over the shop front for years – and chopped it up for fire-wood.
Courtesy Olive Fisher.

also supplied workers in a variety of industries, but managed to secure big contracts with the British Army (when the firm graded thousands of boots after the First World War) and supplied clogs to the railway companies in Hull. The second major confusion between these two clog-makers arose after WWII. In 1949 Leo Brown opened a new shop at No.527 Hessle Road (just two doors from No.531 where Cloggie Walsh had had premises until 1946). It is, therefore, not surprising that the two cloggers became confused in peoples' minds. Indeed, Leo was sometimes wrongly called Cloggie Walsh!

In the WWII interview (mentioned earlier), Abel Griffiths told how each clog was made to suit the customer. The following extract gives a delightful insight into Hessle Road's 'Cloggie Walsh':

> "Many a customer comes in to have a pair made — and stops to see the job done from start to finish. He watches us cut the leather, make his uppers and sees 'em being fastened on to the soles. Happen he has some little peculiarity about his foot, like a corn or summat underneath, so we hollow out the sole to fit him snug. Lots of young women take a bit o' trouble over it and like to have the clog sort of *built* to the foot. The other night I fixed up an A.R.P. [Air Raid Patrol] man with a pair, and housed a beautiful bunion to a nicety. He reckon he'd taken to clogs partly because folks could hear him coming in the blackout..." (p.457).

During the war years, with most of the country's fish being landed on the west coast of Britain, Abel opened a clog shop in Fleetwood. Son Jack stayed in lodgings over there whilst working in the shop and Abel paid him regular visits. But by 1946, with the return of peace and the pick up in trade, larger premises were needed in Hull. The business was moved (from No.531) across the road to No.578 Hessle Road (formerly Mallory's hardware shop on the corner of Hawthorn Avenue — bought for £1000). The advantage here was that it had three bedrooms above the shop. This was helpful in that Abel could live on the premises. He was not so good on his feet as he used to be and, being on the stout side, had difficulties in his latter years with heart problems. 'Cloggie Walsh' died over his beloved shop on 6th May 1955 — he was 73-years old. His funeral service was held at The City Temple on Hessle Road.

The 'age of the clog' was, by this time, almost ended. The demand for fish-dock clogs slowly dwindled. The easier-to-slip-on wellington boots began to replace them. With trade on the decline, Abel's other son, Ron, left clog-making altogether. Jack and Olive continued the Cloggie Walsh business until they retired in October 1964. Olive, who had at first been reluctant to work for a clog-maker, now reflects, "If I had my life all over again, I'd still go to Cloggie Walsh's shop — Hessle Road gets into your blood".

CHAPTER EIGHT

BRIGHTON STREET:
METHODIST MISSION

Hessle Road had many different places of worship. But the Brighton Street Methodist Mission was, for its size, one of the liveliest and most active. Throughout its 83-year history, a hard core of members were filled with a missionary zeal to spread the Christian word to the neighbourhood and beyond.

Before their building opened on 6th March 1889, a small group of Dairycoates railway workers gathered for 'cottage prayer' meetings at various homes in the district. A small shop in Havelock Street was one place where the Primitive Methodists congregated. One of the Mission's earliest founders was Tom Winfield who lived in the Railway Cottages along Trinidad Street. He opened up his house to the Methodists and was their Sunday School teacher for many years. He was succeeded by Superintendents Sykes, Sheen and others.

By the 1880s, Hull was known as "the Metropolis of Primitive Methodism" — a strong-hold of the religion in Britain. The Dairycoates Primitives were determined to establish a place of worship of their own, and so secured a grant from the P/M Chapel Aid Fund. A site was found at the Hessle Road end of the newly-laid-out Brighton Street — near the main road, behind a row of shops. In line with the Primitives' beliefs, their single-story brick building was plain, simple and practical — an all-purpose hall with two small vestries.

From the start, the railway families were the main-spring of the Mission's activities. In the 1880/90s, Dairycoates was a hamlet of railway-workers' cottages. As trawling rapidly expanded, so the railways followed in its wake. The Dairycoates engine-sheds and workshops became the largest on the east coast. The two big railway companies were the London & North Eastern and the Hull & Barnsley Railways. Most of the railway families lived in the crowded terraced houses around Dairycoates, Hawthorn Avenue (formerly Chalk Lane) and, later on, Gipsyville. The Mission drew upon them for members, as well as some fish-dock and trawling families. A few of the remembered names are the Hodsons, Linfords, Hollidays, Watlings, Horsleys and other families.

One Sunday evening, during the First World War, the choir sang with tremendous gusto the anthem "Send Out Thy Light". Suddenly, all the chapel lights went out. Was this a sign from above? No. It was the start of another aerial attack, a 'buzzer night', when all the lights were turned off to black-out the city. Situated close to Hull's major railway complex and docks, Brighton Street was often within range when Zeppelins attacked the port. The Primitives, however, were not easily put off and continued their regular services throughout the bleak war years. Their numbers were obviously reduced and many young men, who served at sea or in the muddy trenches, never re-joined

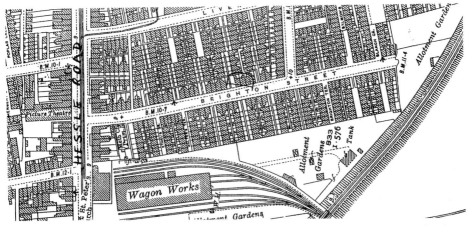

This 1928 map shows the Primitive Methodist chapel at the top north-west side of
Brighton Street – next to the Wagon Works. The Mission, indeed, shared its
fortunes with those of the railways in that many of its members were employed at
the nearby Dairycoates depot. And when the railways declined, so did the Mission.
Courtesy Ordnance Survey.

Brighton Street Mission members regularly gave concerts at their own and other
chapels. The men performed under the name of the "Cures" and the women as the
"Gipsies". When they staged events as a 'mixed group', they were called the
"X.L.'s" (as above c.1930). Performances were usually presented during the winter
months on a Thursday evening.
Courtesy Eddie Reynolds.

their friends in the lively chapel.

The Methodists Union of 1932 brought together most of the Primitives, United, and Wesleyans into one large church. The Brighton Street Primitives joined this uniting move, but its members were determined to continue their evangelical role. Therefore, the old title and tradition of the 'Mission' stayed. It was between the war years that the chapel reached its height and the whole place vibrated with energy: "a dynamic place of worship where the work and witness went out to Hull and the surrounding region".

From the earliest years of the chapel, prayer meetings were paramount. From these sprang a wide variety of groups and activities which benefitted the Hessle Road community as a whole. In the pre- and post-WWII years, members of the Mission took part in a host of events. Each group meeting usually opened with a service in which members took different parts. This particularly happened in the various Christian Endeavour (C/E) groups. These were split into four different sections which covered all ages: Primary (for the under nine-year-olds), Junior (9-13), Young People (13-18), and Senior (18 years and over). The Senior C/E group met on Mondays and were described as "wonderful meetings where many young people began to express themselves".

The Mission building was a dynamic hub of activity which was in use every day of the week. To give an idea of what took place in a 'typical' week during the 1930/40s, the following list has been complied:

MONDAY
Afternoon: Women's Bright Hour
Evening: Senior C/E (18+)
TUESDAY
Evening: Band of Hope + Primary C/E (under 10)
         Young People's C/E (13-18) activities
WEDNESDAY
Evening: Junior C/E (9-13) activities
THURSDAY
Evening: Concert Night or Special Events — almost every other week
         there was a public performance in the winter months
FRIDAY
Evening: Singing practice for the choir
SATURDAY
Volunteers maintained the fabric of the Mission (e.g. improved stage,
         building repairs, etc.)
Sports Day: football, cricket, etc.
SUNDAY
Morning & Afternoon: Sunday School
Morning & Evening: Services included christenings

The Mission had activities for all ages, but especially for the young. Some of the under ten-year olds took part in the Band of Hope devotional services. Originally this was a temperance gathering, where the pledge was signed 'not to be corrupted by the evils of drink' but, as the years passed, its nature changed to include other activities such as practice night for the nativity play. The Young Peoples' Christian Endeavour eventually became the focal point for all the chapel's youth activities. An inevitable outcome of the Mission's social events was that there were many romances, followed by a number of marriages — held at the chapel, of course.

Courtship was a very tentative process in the 1930s. Young Frank Lindo was determined to bring himself to the attention of Gertrude Robinson — the apple-of-his-eye. He deliberately waited for her to pass through the Mission's main doorway as people left the Sunday evening service. Frank then ardently wished her a direct and forceful "Good Night". He did this regularly and on the third Sunday even managed to shake Gertrude by the hand. The next week Frank got up enough courage to ask her to walk along with him to Pickering Park after the service. This they did together for the next six Sundays; regardless of the fact that every November Sunday evening (1934) the heavens opened and they got drenched to the skin. But the flame of love, once kindled, could not be dowsed by any downpour. On 2nd August 1937 Frank married his sweetheart Gertrude at the chapel (see photo).

In the late 1930s a Boys' Group was formed which met every Tuesday evening. The organisers begged a small billiard table and various games' equipment for one of the small vestries. The boys had "a great, if somewhat crowded, time". During the Second World War these Tuesday sessions were opened to the girls too. It was mainly girls who made up the 'Eager Beavers', with pianist Doris Devine. They regularly performed at old peoples' homes and, on occasions, in the Fishermen's Bethel during their charity concerts for the families of trawlermen lost at sea.

Youngsters at the Mission were central to the Sunday activities. In addition to the morning and evening services (when christenings were performed), there was the children's Sunday School in the afternoon. This was well-attended, especially between the wars with over 150 scholars. Those who ran the Sunday School were affectionately known as "auntie" or "uncle".

In 1934, the Mission began its Sunday School Festivals: an 'original venture which others [chapels and churches] followed' — they ran each year over three evenings in June. The girls predominated in this festivity. The retiring Sunday School Queen (with a crown of blue forget-me-nots) handed over to the new Queen (with a gold and pearl cut-glass crown). Each Queen had a large retinue of smartly-dressed attendants. The chorus "Hail, Our Queen" rang out and speeches were made. Afterwards, a top boy was made Captain and the lads entertained with sketches. Maypole Braiding and singing rounded off this annual festival (with its strong pagan roots). Every year the Brighton Street May Queen was entered for the title of Sunday School Queen along with other girls from all over Hull in the May Festival.

Other annual events were the Summer Camp visits to Muston, near Filey (begun after WWII). The camp was on a farm and everyone had duties: some shopped, others cooked, or did jobs around the farm. Well-remembered is a local character who the youngsters nicknamed 'Desperate Dan'. His twice-weekly (smelly) job was to collect waste from the toilets. On Sundays the Mission teenagers attended the Filey Fishermen's Chapel (in the late-1940s).

On 2nd August 1937, Frank Lindo married his sweet-heart Gertrude Robinson at the Brighton Street Methodist Mission. Railway worker Frank, although not a regular worshipper at the chapel, specifically attended in order to come into contact with Gertrude. Her boss at the hardware shop drove the newly-weds in his car to Scarborough where the Lindo's had their honeymoon.
Courtesy Gertrude & Frank Lindo.

Mission members took part in various sporting activities. A chapel-based football team was formed long before the Great War and played in Church and other local leagues. In this early-1930s team are four of the Stone brothers (Sid, David, Albert and Isaac). It seems they joined the church more to score goals than save souls.
Courtesy Eddie Reynolds.

Many of the mums and Mission women did the dress-making for the annual May Queen event; but a key person at these times was tailoress Emily Tutty who lived near the chapel. The festivities were actually held in June over a three-day period from 1934 onwards. The 1946 May Queen was Thelma Harling of Gipsyville (above). Courtesy Mary Kilvington.

For a sixteen-year period after the 1939-45 War, the Mission arranged an annual holiday at the Muston Farm Camp for their teenagers. At nearby Filey, five Hessle Road girls enjoy their ice-cream and a stroll along the sea-front (1949): Mary Fullerton, Betty Farrow, Sylvia Meanwell, Rose Fullerton, and Dorothy Crosser. Courtesy Mary Kilvington.

These local men all wore navy-blue guernseys and black sea-boots — they were renowned for their lively singing. For some boys and girls this was the only chance of a holiday.

Each December, the youngsters presented to packed audiences their annual three-night Christmas Pantomime. The Mission Methodists were keen concert-givers — usually staged in the winter months on a Thursday evening at the chapel. "The Cures" — known as the 'single-men's effort' — were formed in the late 1920s and continued well into the 1930s. They also entertained at other churches throughout the city — dressed as pierrots. They described themselves, perhaps a little tongue-in-cheek in those years of the Great Depression, as "the Lads who make Life worth Living". There was good-natured rivalry between the lads and their female counter-part, "The Gipsies", who "added their sparkle to the events". In another routine, the women dressed up as Dutch Girls with long plaits. From these two groups were formed a small mixed group who went under the name of the "X.L.'s". Their self-penned sketches were presented first at their own chapel and later at other venues in the East Riding. Sometimes they went across the Humber on the old paddle-steamer to Lincolnshire. They performed until the outbreak of war in 1939.

Saturday was the big day for sport, with home matches mainly at Costello playing fields (in the latter years). Both the football and cricket teams were established before WWI and competed in church and local leagues. After the Second World War the Mission had two teams in the Methodist Cricket League which they championed several times. A girls' net-ball team started after WWII — their matches were mainly held in the evenings. Within the chapel itself the youngsters played a range of indoor games such as table-tennis, snooker, billiards, and Lexicon (a spelling card-game).

The choir was one of the Mission's oldest and strongest groups. At its height there were forty singers. They often helped out at functions for other churches. Friday evenings were set aside for choir practice conducted, over the years, by a succession of competent masters: Playfoot, Rea, Kirby, Devine, and Reynolds. Eddie Reynolds conducted for around forty years (excluding his WWII service) and his wife Alice was organist between 1931 and 1972. She played there from being twelve-years old. People still remember the equally long-serving Mrs. Giles who was organist until 1919. She and her husband had a wet fish shop on Hessle Road. Prior to a serious illness Mrs. Giles taught Ivy Winfield to play the organ and she took over as Mission organist when she was thirteen-years old. Ivy left after about ten years and went on to become a private music teacher in the city. One of the highlights of the choir's year (post-WWII) was the Good Friday Cantata. On these occasions they were assisted by members of other church choirs and some of Hull's finest vocalists.

The unsung, behind-the-scenes workers — who kept most of the Mission's activities going — were the chapel women such as Ann Raper, and lay preacher Mary Holroyd. A thirty-strong group met every Monday afternoon as the Women's Bright Hour. They began with a short service, followed by an outside speaker, e.g., from the Salvation Army, and other bodies.

Those involved with the Mission speak with pride of former members who had "gone out from their ranks" to become ministers, lay preachers, Sunday

School teachers, or church officials in Hull and elsewhere in England, Scotland, Wales, Africa, New Zealand, and the USA.

By the early 1970s the fate of the Mission looked bleak. The railways were being axed and the fishing industry had lost another Cod War. Decline and decay also affected the neighbourhood. Brighton Street, once crowded with children at play, slowly emptied as families were moved to far-away modern estates (like North Hull and Bransholme). Mission membership dropped as "many chapels felt the draught". The trustees decided to put their building up for sale (it was later purchased by Hull Corporation). A camaraderie grew between the chapel officials and the last-to-leave Brighton Street residents who often called out, "Any news about the Mission?"

The last service was held on the 12th May, 1972 (conducted by Reverend George H. Turner). It was "packed to the doors as people rejoiced in the glorious history of the Mission". So strong is the members' devotion toward the Brighton Street Methodist Church, that they hold an annual re-union every year (on the nearest Saturday evening to the 12th May). These are full of lively chatter as people reminisce about when their vibrant chapel was in its heyday. At the 1990 re-union, one elderly lady recalled how her mother used to tell her, "I should take your bed to the Mission if I were you — you spend most of your time there!".

*This late-1930s picture of the **Kitty** shows her with an open-bridge. Charles and his father, Herbert Ayre, often got soaked to the skin. Charles recalled that "we would then have our clothes dry on us before we got home". Despite this, and more severe conditions, Charles never suffered rheumatism. In the background is Pickering's **Lord Hailsham** (H.82) trawler which was torpedoed during an E-boat attack in the English Channel on 27th February, 1943 on Admiralty service.*
Courtesy Charles Ayre.

*Charles Ayre aboard his motor launch **Kitty** which was moored in the Humber Dock Basin. He lived in nearby Wellington Street (No.4) and was on 24-hour call. If a storm suddenly blew up at night, Charles sailed the vessel away from the quay wall to prevent her being smashed to pieces. He often had to wait a couple of hours for the weather to calm before he could return ashore. The **Kitty** was named by Herbert after his youngest daughter (born in 1920).*
Courtesy Charles Ayre.

70

CHAPTER NINE

KITTY:
RIVER TAXI

It is well known that taxis were an important part of a trawlerman's activities while ashore. But less is known about Hull's river taxi, *Kitty*, which also served the trawling industry and crewmen in various ways. At high tide, for example, *Kitty* was on standby in the Humber outside the lockgates of St. Andrew's Fish Dock. This was in case a trawler, which had to catch the tide, was not fully manned. *Kitty* was then hired to take late-comers to the vessel anchored in the Humber. She did this and other work for nearly fifty years from the 1920s onward.

The 39-foot motor launch belonged to the Ayre family and was sailed by father and son: Herbert and Charles. The family business was run from No.4 Wellington Street — near the Humber Dock Basin where *Kitty* was berthed. The job demanded that Charles was on call 24-hours a day. Many a night his wife and two daughters were disturbed when he had to attend a trawler in the estuary.

The demands for *Kitty's* services were beyond that of just taking late-comers out to the trawlers. Charles was hired by ship-builders, such as Cook, Welton & Gemmell of Beverley, when brand new trawlers were put through their paces. About thirty or so specialists were ferried back and forth throughout the day. During these trials, and at other times, compass adjusters carried out their work in the Humber. Charles transported different adjusters from Castles, Cooks, Pearsons and, in later years, the Compass Department of the Hull Trawlers Mutual Insurance. Marine photographers Barnard & Straker hired Herbert and his boat to take pictures (for postcards) of trawlers and cargo boats as they plied the river. Barnard is remembered as a small Jewish deaf-mute who later inherited a fortune and left Hull for London. At other times, if the Humber ferry was out of action, Charles took copies of the Hull Daily Mail across to the south bank, along with stranded passengers.

In 1927 *Kitty* was modified to take passengers on pleasure trips on the Humber during the summer months. Meanwhile, with a larger vessel, Herbert got the lucrative contract from a flying school to 'shepherd' (tow) flying-boats in the Humber off Brough Aerodrome (1920s-1939).

The treacherous Humber — for which Charles had a deep respect — also provided *Kitty* with a fair degree of salvage and rescue work. A tragic trawler loss occurred on 9th January 1935 when the *Edgar Wallace* (H.262) 'turned turtle' off Hessle (see Chapter 5). In the weeks that followed, the *Kitty* took out a team of Grimsby divers; but they failed to raise this Newington trawler. The attempt was jinxed, even a salvage tug foundered during the work and its engineer drowned.

The *Kitty* came close to a perilous end itself when another Hull trawler went down in the Humber. It was the stormy night of 11th December 1938 when Charles was urgently contacted by an anxious insurance agent and the ships' husband for the Yorkshire Steam Fishing Company. Their trawler *Reefflower* (H.86) 'fell across' (hit) a Goole ship which was at anchor. It was believed — as happened three years earlier with the *Edgar Wallace* — that the crew were still helplessly adrift on the trawler and their lives were in danger. In the black night the *Kitty* was swept down river by the raging tide. As they raced 'hell for leather', the three men strained their eyes as they peered into the blackness for the lights of the distressed vessel. Unknowingly, the *Kitty* passed over the wreck of the foundered *Reefflower* — not far from St. Andrew's Dock. At Hessle Haven, they put ashore to telephone the owner's office and heard that all the crew had got safely ashore near Riverside Quay. Charles recalled that on their journey back, *Kitty* must have missed the wreck for the second time that evening.

A German salvage team failed to raise the *Reefflower* or, later, the *Lady Jeanette* (H.466) which went down in March 1939. Charles noticed how the engineers listened avidly to Hitler's speeches broadcast from Nazi Germany and sang patriotic songs. Indeed, when war was declared a few months later, they immediately abandoned the nearly-completed salvage work and dashed home to join the forces.

Charlie was a legend on the Humber. He knew the tricky estuary like the back of his hand — in day or night-time, in bright or fog-bound conditions. In pre-radar days, Charles adopted an ancient system to find his way around in dangerous fog. He described the technique as "You would blow a mouth-horn and listen for its echo. As it came back to you, you calculated the distance you were from the land".

His instinctive gift to navigate the unforgiving Humber held him in good stead during the Second World War, and enabled him to avoid military call up. In the black of night he guided both British and Icelandic trawlers from the mouth of the estuary, near Spurn Point, straight to St. Andrew's Fish Dock. Obviously, the vessels were blacked out to avoid being spotted by the Luftwaffe on regular bombing missions when they used the Humber as a major landmark to direct them on their raids into the heart of northern England. The trawler skipper had a man positioned on the bow to signal up to the bridge as he received directions from the *Kitty*.

Charles Ayre was exempt from war service because his job was classed as a 'reserved occupation'. Owen Hellyer of the trawler firm (who was also well-placed within the Ministry of Agriculture, Food & Fisheries) wrote a letter to the War Department which ensured that Charles would not be drafted into the forces. The letter argued that without the work of the *Kitty* the fragile remains of the Hull fishing industry would completely collapse. Another war-time role of the *Kitty* was when she was employed by DEMIS. An officer from the Defensibly Equipped Merchant Service was regularly taken aboard civilian ships for him to test their anti-aircraft guns. Charles waited while all the guns were "shot off wildly", and then got the signal to return the 'gunman' ashore. On one occasion Charles was called to a ship near Alexandra Dock. The next

At high water the Humber was often crowded with shipping and in its most dangerous state, especially when there was a strong spring tide. Accidents were frequent and the **Kitty** was employed in a variety of jobs. In this print from the Ayre postcard collection is the **Lady Beryl** (H.283) whose anchor chain fouled the propeller of the **Alexandrite** (H.11). They drifted ashore near Victoria Dock and ended up in this incredible position (c.1930).
Courtesy Charles Ayre.

The **Loch Torridon** (H.165), after a collision in the Humber, beached near Alexandra Dock (c.1951?). The crew struggled ashore watched by scores of on-lookers. One of the shipwrecked men recalled that none offered to help: "had they been Hessle Roaders, they'd have been down to give a hand straight away". The **Kitty** played a role in the successful salvage operation. The tug in this picture is the **Boatman** which was involved in the **Edgar Wallace** (H.262) incident.
Courtesy Charles Ayre.

73

*The two-year old **Lady Jeanette** (H.466) sank in the Humber on 8th March 1939 off Hessle foreshore after her anchor-chain broke in a strong running tide – nine of her crew died. **Kitty** was employed in the salvage work carried out by a team of German engineers. They had raised the wreck, almost to the surface, when war broke out. The patriotic Nordics immediately abandoned the work and let the **Jeanette** sink to the bottom again – thereby denying Britain a potential war trawler.*
Courtesy Charles Ayre (Cartlidge print).

day, there was news that a Humber keel had been blown up; it was only then he realised that *Kitty* had been moored over the same mine (dropped by the Luftwaffe).

Being a small firm, the Ayres depended mainly upon the fishing industry for their livelihood, and so bent to the whims of the trawler owners. Whether or not a trawler was due to sail, Charles was·outside St. Andrew's lockpit just in case *Kitty's* services were required. When Hull fishing was depleted in WWII, Charles asked trawler-owner Tom Boyd, "Can we change the attendance arrangements?". The reply was a firm, "No". Charles, therefore, was available purely on speck and earned nothing if he was not needed. It was this sort of attitude which ensured that Herbert Ayre never drove his car onto the Fish Dock. He was afraid the owners might think he made too much money out of them and so end their business with him.

Over the years, Charles maintained a good relationship with the Humber Pilots in that they had a mutual system of freely helping each other. As a trained engineer, Charles repaired the engines of the pilots' boats; and they, in turn, sometimes took late crewmen out to the trawlers whilst he had a night off with his family.

After WWII the *Kitty* was employed in more salvage work. The Humber claimed the *St. Leander* (H.19) in January 1951 after a collision with the Hull trawler *Davy* (H.213). Charles knew the Humber well and guessed, from experience, that the salvage operation would be a waste of time, effort and money. He was aware that silt rapidly collected in a sunken hulk, and that a wreck soon settled heavily into the muddy bottom. The weight of the vessel doubled or trebled and it became impossible to shift. When the engineers themselves reached this conclusion, they usually blew the top of the trawler clean off with dynamite so the hull was sucked down into the mud forever. Two other Humber incidents in the 1950s, the *Loch Torridon* (H.165) and *Stella Carina* (H.355), however, were both successfully re-floated.

Charles' regular job, the transport of late-comers out to the trawlers, was not as simple as it sounds. The key problem stemmed from drunkenness. The men were usually late because the ships' runner had probably tracked them down in a Hessle Road pub or wherever. Sometimes a trawler might have waited several hours before Charles was asked to taxi a crewman aboard. Meanwhile, some of the crew already on board had sobered up and realised they had left behind some unfinished personal business which urgently needed attention at home. So when Charles brought out the final crewman to get the ship underway, two others might leap into his boat and demand to go ashore. Despite the skipper's curses, some men refused to leave *Kitty* and were taken back to dry land.

Obviously, these antics put Charles in an awkward position and it did not please the owners who received his bill for the cost to ferry the men back and forth (the firms, as usual, deducted this charge from the men's settling pay). Charles, however, formulated a solution to this problem. He began to approach the trawler dead centre of the stern before he came alongside, so as not to be seen. The man and his heavy sea bag were usually aboard before reluctant crewmen realised the *Kitty* had made a fast getaway. This crafty move, however, was not easy if a crewman was drunk. Conversely, frustrated men aboard the trawler sometimes 'jumped ship' (literally) and leapt overboard into the water so that the *Kitty* would have to pick them up. Sometimes men feigned illness when they saw *Kitty* approach. This put the skipper in a quandary because he dare not risk it if the man was genuinely ill — so again, a crewman might come ashore. Drunkards unnerved Charles when they threw his life-belts over the side. At other times, even a skipper came late 'a little worse for wear' after his time ashore. Yet Charles was sympathetic and knew that the trawlermen "played hard because they worked hard".

One deckhand, indeed, decided to have a joke at the expense of the ships' runner. Charles was confronted by a very large crewman held up by two men. When they put him aboard *Kitty* he collapsed in a heap. Charles, not a big man himself, said he would be unable to get him onto the trawler alone, and so the two runners came along to do the job. As it happened, the trawler was at the Saltend terminal being filled with oil. The helpless man, therefore, had to be carried up a steep ladder onto the jetty. A rope was fastened around his waist with Charles up top to take the slack and the two runners below to struggle as best they could. When all three took the strain, the big man suddenly sprang into life, shot up the ladder, leapt onto the trawler, and laughed loudly. Charles did not know the name of this joker, but I wonder if it was the famous 'Dillinger' (see Chapter 14).

As well as getting certain vessels away, there is a story of a trawler on its return from the distant fishing grounds. It had just missed the high tide and so was too late to enter St. Andrew's Fish Dock. The skipper, therefore, had to anchor for twelve hours in the Humber to await the next high water. As the ship's cook was almost out of food, he decided to give his crew a special treat. He asked Charlie to go ashore to bring back twenty-one lots of fish and chips. The fish fryer was delighted and inquired who wanted such a big order. He thought it was a joke and refused to believe that it was for a trawler full of fresh cod and haddock.

In 1973, after forty-eight years on the Humber, Charles sold *Kitty* and retired. This gave him time to develop his artistic talents in sculpture, poetry, and music, as well as his engineering interests. Sadly, Charles died suddenly at home on 17th December 1989 aged eighty-eight. It was a pity that he was unable to complete the memoirs he was writing of his extraordinary life on the Humber.

He had a lovable sense of humour, and guarded a number of surprising secrets. These might have startled some of the people he ferried about on the dangerous Humber. He was almost totally colour-blind, so could not make out the different ships' lights at night. He was a very poor swimmer, so could never dive overboard to save anyone. He was not a Hull man, but was born in the rival port of Grimsby (1901) and moved to the north bank as a child in 1906. He never employed anyone else to repair his boats. And he *never* took out any insurance for his passengers, himself or his beloved *Kitty*!

*The 440-ton **Stella Carina** (H.573) was holed amidships on her portside by the collier **Mendip** in the Humber (March 1959). Skipper Fred Sullivan and engineer George Roberts (up to his waist in water) skilfully drove her up the stony bank between Victoria Dock and Earle's yard. All the crew were rescued by a pilot cutter and the fire-boat. The salvage work took 77 days to complete and the **Carina** was back fishing at the deep-sea grounds within six months of the collision. Courtesy Charles Ayre.*

*Hellyer's 575-ton Shakespearean-class trawler **Macbeth** (H.113) was the setting for
the strong taboo about 'grunters'. Pighides were wrongly placed on board, the
skipper went berserk and ordered the men to throw the hides in the Humber to
avoid a curse being placed on the voyage. The 1938 **Macbeth** came to no harm at
sea and she ended her days at the scrap-yard in 1966. This is a subsequent **Macbeth**
(H.201) trawler which I took in St.Andrew's Fish Dock during a strike in 1974.
Copyright Alec Gill.*

CHAPTER TEN

GRUNTER:
TRAWLING TABOO

Of the scores of taboo words which must never be uttered aboard Hull trawlers, the most feared was PIG. If someone had to mention the creature, its actual name was not spoken because that "tempted Providence". Instead, it was either spelt out letter by letter "P-I-G" or an alternative was used such as "grunter", "curly-tail", "porker", or the "four-footed beastie".

One account which illustrates this strong, wide-spread taboo relates to the Hull trawler *Macbeth* (H.113) as it set off for the White Sea fishing grounds in the late 1940s. She was running-off down the Humber as the men cleared the decks of stores and battened down the hatches for the outward voyage. From his wheelhouse the skipper watched the men untie the parcel of hides. These were used to cover the hatches and protect the trawl net on the rough seabed. Among the cowhides was a pigskin. The 'old man' went berserk and, with lots of foul language, ordered the men to throw the pighide overboard immediately.

Another story is told of a skipper who owned a small-holding at Ferriby (west of Hull) where he kept swine and once took some piglets to sea. His intention was to kill the animals for fresh meat during the voyage — to give the crew a treat. Perhaps he was not superstitious and was unaware of the implications, or just wanted to test the crew and observe their reactions. Some of the trawlermen, however, were very unhappy and the murmurings of discontent grew to an uproar.

It must be added that it was not only trawlermen in Hull who were so fearful of anything to do with the four-footed beastie. Anson (1932) described how "pig" is a taboo word all around the British coast, especially in Cornwall, Yorkshire, and Scotland — "There is no animal more unlucky for fishermen" and few put to sea after seeing one (p.63). Around the turn of the century, at Aberdeen, a dismal fishing trip was blamed on the fact that a piece of ham had been taken aboard. Eventually, the cook of the steam trawler threw the meat into the sea. A mischievous Scottish lad once flung a sow's tail aboard a fishing boat as it headed out of Buckhaven. The vessel immediately turned back and the crew refused to sail until the next day (Radford, 1975, p.265).

In Brixham, home of Hull's earliest smack-owning families, local fishermen never carried pork to sea (Opie & Tatem, 1989). It may well have been the Devonshire fishing families who brought most of the ancient superstitions with them; and the beliefs spread from ship to ship, and from street to street.

The 'pig' taboo was perhaps stronger aboard the Hull trawlers than it was in the Hessle Road fishing community. This seems to be the case because it was not unknown for some families to keep a pig-sty — those, that is, who had a long garden or good-sized backyard. In Beecroft Street, three households kept curly-tails, as well as chickens, goats, and geese. Neighbours saved their potato peelings, stale bread, and left-overs for the animals. Whenever a new litter was born, children from the street were delighted to see the pink piglets and hear them squeal. Come market day, the youngsters were roped in to help herd the fully-grown grunters into a cart — horse-drawn in the early days. They blocked off passage-ends to direct the swine towards the street. There, others stood on the pavement with boards to guide the frightened creatures up a ramp, with trawl nets on the sides, into the cart. Division Road was another pig-keeping street, and so was Glasgow Street — as described by Ernest Crowther in his Malet Lambert autobiography (1987, No.36). He told how the kids 'accidentally' let the pigs run loose into the street and of the excitement as they tried to get them back.

Although grunters were kept in the fishing community, this is not to say that Hessle Roaders did not have any anti-pig superstitions. Recently, I met a group of women who still adamantly refused to utter the animal's name. The nearest one came to it was to spell out, in a mouthed whisper, "P-I-G". Another woman held up both hands to show that her fingers were firmly crossed. This 'protected' her from the harmful effects of having heard the forbidden word. She would not even spell out the name. Apparently, the harmful effects of hearing the taboo word can be averted by touching cold iron — in a similar way to 'touching wood'.

If the question is asked, "Why is it so wrong to say the word 'pig'?" — the usual answer is "I don't know". The fear has been passed on from parents with no explanation other than the dire warning that harm will follow if the word is spoken aloud. So why this fear and dread of grunters by Hull and other fishermen? Research into the source of this superstitious belief led in two opposite directions: Christian and Pagan.

In both the Old and New Testaments, the Bible is riddled with anti-pig comments. Leviticus warns the children of Israel, "You must not eat their [pigs] meat or touch their carcasses; they are unclean for you" (11:7). This advice might be based on health grounds. That is, to prevent infection from parasitic tapeworm. If infected pork is under-cooked and gets into the human stomach, the tapeworm feeds on the food, and can grow to over three feet in length. Cysticercosis is very serious and there is no specific treatment — even today. One sympton is epileptic attacks and, if unchecked, the disease causes madness. Also at the medical level, it was once believed that a bite from a pig caused cancer. Furthermore, if someone ate its cooked brains, folklore held that they would speak the truth. The Devil is also part of this superstition in that both the pig and Satan (apparently) have cloven feet.

The most direct Biblical link between grunters and mariners relates to the healing work of Christ. Jesus and the Gadarene Swine is a story which specifically mentions *drowning*. Christ had just landed by boat on the side of a lake when a mad man fell on his knees before him. Legion, the crazed man, lived in a Roman soldiers' grave-yard and was possessed by evil spirits. The demons pleaded with Jesus, "Send us among the pigs". He did this and the large herd of about 2000 "rushed down the steep bank into the lake and were drowned" (Mark 5:1-13). It has been suggested that the trawlermen therefore avoid the word 'pig' because of this Biblical link with drowning. So to avoid being lost at sea, the trawlermen avoided the word 'pig'. Christianity, therefore, provides *some* reasons why fishermen should be wary of the animal. A totally different picture of grunter emerges, however, if we look back at the longer-established Pagan beliefs.

The view here is generally more favourable toward the creature. And the associated mythology stretches as far afield from Iceland to India. The long-ago ancestor of the farm-yard pig was the wild boar. Generally, they were feared for their vicious ferocity — a dangerous quarry which sometimes got the better of the hunters. In Norse folklore the boar represents the souls of the departed which are believed to stir up the storm clouds during Odin's wild hunt. In Celtic mythology, especially in Wales and Ireland, the pig is revered as a god (re: Mabinogion). Sir James Frazer (1922), in his highly-esteemed, twelve-volume tome *The Golden Bough*, studied the role of the pig in ancient Europe as a sacred cornspirit.

Interestingly enough, other taboo words of the Hull trawlermen, such as 'hare', 'cat', and 'rabbit' are also cornspirits of our ancestors. Cornspirits are central to Pagan beliefs which, in turn, are deeply involved with the forces of nature (as are the fishermen on the wild waters). At harvest, as the reapers scythed the last few sheafs, they sometimes saw a wild boar dash from the field. They believed this to be the transformed spirit of the crop about to flee the land. They captured the boar, killed it, and offered it as a sacrifice to Mother Earth. This was not only a 'thanks giving', but also a way to ensure a good crop the next year. The ashes were ceremoniously scattered on the fields and some mixed with the seeds before they were sown (is there a link, indeed, between 'sow the land' and 'sow' for female pig?). The last sheaf itself (referred to as 'the sow') was saved and baked into a boar-shaped loaf. This was later placed on the farmer's Yule-tide table throughout the Winter festivities. Only during the Spring sowing season was it eaten by the sowers and ploughman. And part was mixed with the corn seeds to ensure a healthy crop in the harvest. And so the cyclic seasons passed by from year to year with a strong ritual which revolved around the sacred pig.

This is, I'm afraid, a simplified account of Frazer's grand work. He goes on to argue how the Greeks mythologized the pig into the god-figures of Demeter, Attis, and Adonis; while for the Egyptians the animal was associated with Osiris. Frazer also claimed that the Jewish view of swine, as being "unclean", had its origins in reverence rather than revulsion. Even the Greek author Plutarch was curious over this point. In Pagan times, then, the pig was a holy creature endowed with supernatural god-like powers. Ordinary mortals, especially among the lowest-order, felt compelled to avoid any direct contact with the sacred being. *And even to utter its name was forbidden.*

The Hull trawlermen's 20th century taboo might, then, be a relic of this powerful Pagan view, based upon the belief that the pig was a god. This attitude is perhaps best summed up by an expression often used by Hull trawler-mate Carr who used to say, "I'm not scared of man nor beast, apart from pig".

One final trawling incident related to grunter concerns a trip aboard the *James Barrie* (H.15). Whenever the mate John Evans saw a piece of pork being

Not all trawlermen avoided links with grunter. One of Hull's most decorated war-time skippers, 'Mad' Rilatt, carried this lucky pig amulet with him from around 1912. It is a small match-holder (note the strip underneath on which to strike a match) lent to me by his daughter-in-law Laura. It worked as a lucky charm for him because he survived active service in both world wars (see Chapter 3).
Copyright Alec Gill.

*Superstitions are not easy to illustrate. Can someone be photographed **NOT** doing something? Nevertheless, there is some evidence of our ancient pig taboo in Britain in the shape of this **Blue Boar** pub sign in Chipping Norton. Hull trawlermen are in the company of royalty in their respect for the pig. King Richard III and the Earl of Oxford (their heraldic shields are in the top right-hand corner of the sign) wore armour emblazoned with boar symbols. They hoped to acquire the ferocity and courage of this sovereign of all beasts.*
Copyright Alec Gill.

brought up from the fish room (where it had been stored on the ice during the outward trip) he cursed and swore, "Here comes some bad luck". Skipper Bernard Stipetic heard him one day and said, "I'll cure you of that silly superstition". He cut off the sow's tail and tied it to the headline of a new trawl just before it was shot away. The *James Barrie* had not towed more than fifteen minutes when Bang, Bang, both warps parted! From that day forth, this top Hull skipper never allowed pork aboard any of his trawlers again.

*Top Hull skipper Bernard Stipetic of the **James Barrie** (H.15) was not a superstitious man; whereas his mate John Evans was very wary of anything to do with "P-I-G". The skipper lost some very expensive trawl gear in his attempt to cure Evans of his 'silly superstition'. A number of years later, the 666-ton **James Barrie** (ex.Benella) sank on 29th March 1969 in the Pentland Firth while in tow after being stranded on Louther Skerry (Orkneys). This does not, however, mean there was a link between "P-I-G" and the loss of the trawler.*
Copyright Malcolm Fussey.

CHAPTER ELEVEN

MOHICAN:
WRECKED IN ICELAND

During 1939, before the war started, Hull had three peace-time trawler losses. These were *Lady Jeanette* (H.466), *St. Delphine* (H.380) and *Mohican* (H.391). The first two are well-known in the port because both incidents occurred in the Humber within two days of each other in March. Less is known about the *Mohican* which ran aground at Iceland a month later.

The steam trawler *Mohican* was considered 'unlucky'. "She was a dirty old ship which took seas unnecessarily", said Stephen Mahoney who was, at that time, a 22-year-old sparehand. Stephen, nicknamed 'Big Steve' or 'Lofty' because he was so tall, had seen a run of five different skippers before Thomas R.W. Miller took charge of the *Mohican*. Perhaps because of her being a 'bad sea ship', skippers were quick to ditch her. Big Steve described the crew as "a good set of fine men". The eight-year old *Mohican* was built in 1931 at Beverley by Cook, Welton & Gemmell. Her specifications were 374 tons gross, 152 net, 146 feet long (Official No. 162256; Port No. 54/1931, Hull registration H.391). This coal-burner belonged to Hellyer Brothers and was one of their tribal-named trawlers. Others in this fleet at that time were: *Bengali* (H.397), *Dervish* (H.249), *Esquimaux* (H.29), *Norse* (H.348), and *Spaniard* (H.404).

The *Mohican's* fatal trip began on the 5th April when she left Hull for the fishing grounds off the south-west coast of Iceland. Thirteen days later, the fish-rooms were more or less full. The skipper — "a gentleman" — had done well on his first trip with the *Mohican*. He decided to make just a couple more hauls off Portland Light before heading home. Instead of going around the outside of the Vestmannaeyjar (Westman) Islands, a course was set between 'Lion Rocks' and the mainland. Normally, this 'shortcut' is safe because there is plenty of water between them. On the 18th April, however, an on-shore wind was blowing hard.

"There was a slight shudder; then suddenly, she was thrown over. We had touched the bottom", recalled Stephen. All the boards flew over the deck to the fo'c'sle. Down below in the engine-room the fire doors were flung open as she laid over. Despite her reputation as a 'bad sea ship', she managed to right herself and the engineers were signalled to put the engine into reverse. But she would not budge. The *Mohican* was stuck fast ashore and took all the seas broadside on. The crew were stranded on Rangar Sands, east of Stokkseyri. This is a wide area of black sand or, to be precise, volcanic ash — not a "sandy beach" as described in the Hull newspapers of the time.

The skipper ordered all portholes to be tightly fastened and hatches battened down. This done, most of the crew huddled in the highest part of the trawler — the wheelhouse. Except, that is, for the engineers and firemen who managed

*This dark and damaged print of the **Mohican** (H.391), taken a couple of days after the rescue of the crew in April 1939, shows her ashore at Iceland during the salvage operation. In the foreground are some of the farmers (with their dogs) who got the trawlermen safely ashore. They unloaded coal from the vessel in order to make her lighter. On the horizon is the Icelandic gunboat **Aegir**.*
Courtesy Stephen Mahoney.

*This is an old photograph of Portland Head on the south coast of Iceland. It was taken by Percy Ross of the trawler firm F. & T. Ross in August 1904. It was near Portland that the **Mohican** (H.391) went aground on the black volcanic ash of Ranger Sands – a dangerous stretch of the coast beset with bogs, marshes and quick-sand.*
Courtesy Kevin Marshall.

to keep 'a bit of steam in the boilers' (essential, as it happened, for the crew's eventual escape).

Outside, the *Mohican* was pounded by every incoming wave. Some crashed down over the ship and washed right along from the stern up to the whaleback (bow). Despite this, the crew managed to launch distress flares. These were not necessary as it happened. Their plight had been watched by farmers on ponies who had spotted the trawler close to land before it got into difficulty. Dawn had just broken (0500 hours) when the trawlermen caught sight of the Icelanders. Communications were impossible because of the wide distance, deafening seas, and language differences. Nevertheless, the human urge to save others over-rode these obstacles.

The Icelandic farmers found the *Mohican's* Carley float washed up on the shore. It had been swept overboard in the gale. The *Hull Times* (22nd April 1939) correctly reported the loss of this piece of life-saving equipment. The short article then went on to report that the Icelanders fired a rocket to the *Mohican* and got the crew off by breeches buoy. This account is false. It was, instead, the trawlermen who fired a rocket to the shore.

The farmers drew in the thin line which had a thicker rope attached. They secured this firmly to the washed-up float. Before they gave the signal for the Hull men to haul it back, a second rope was tied to the rear of the Carley. With a line fixed to either end of the raft, the plan was to ferry the crewmen from the stricken trawler to the shore by a floating pulley-like system. The *Mohican* used its steam-driven winch-gear during this critical operation.

It was decided that deckie-learner Morgan of Gillett Street and fireman Bill Dale (25) of Tadman Street be the first to leave in the Carley float. This life-saving apparatus, it must be stressed, was not the height of luxury. Trawlers, unlike Merchant Navy 'big boats', were not required by law to carry lifeboats. Paying lip-service to safety, the owners did fit many of their deep-sea trawlers with a Carley float. This was simply an oval-shaped cork ring. It had no cover, so there was no protection overhead; and no bottom, except a piece of rope netting. Its sole purpose was to act, as the name suggests, as a 'float' (invented by someone called Carley — perhaps for the Royal Navy).

The deckie and fireman leapt into the Carley and were immediately tossed out. Their combined weight was not enough to keep the float steady in the rough waters. After they were rescued from their ordeal, four other men struggled onto the ring to try *their* luck. Their combined weight was enough to keep it stable in the choppy waves. The Icelanders then heaved in the life-raft. After the first four scrambled ashore, the empty float was winched back by the *Mohican*.

As the sea continued its mighty roar, two further hauls brought three men each time. This then left four of the fourteen crew still aboard: skipper Miller, mate Mayes, bosun Jenkinson, and Big Steve. Theirs was the most tricky exit because there was no one left aboard the abandoned *Mohican* to steady the float with a line as it bobbed about. Consequently, the Carley got thrown right up the beach by the fast running surf. Apart from a few cuts and bruises, everyone was alright. The crewmen were chilled to the bone in their saturated clothes and that long stretch of Iceland's south coast is beset with marshes, quick-sand and bogs. Under the guidance of the Icelandic farmers, however, the bedraggled men were led to safety. To get out of the bitter cold and into the warmth of the farms, a few miles away, the crew had to pony-trek — an unusual form of transport for these seafarers.

At the farmstead — nothing more than two or three small shacks — the first thing the men got was a bath. They stripped naked — "there was no modesty, we had to get our clothes off so they could be dried. We were forever washing the black volcanic ash out of our hair", said Lofty. After their bath in the natural hot spring waters of Iceland, the men tucked into a wonderful cooked meal, and then had a welcomed rest. Neighbours all pitched in to help the men recover. "The Icelanders could not do enough for us." They were not rich, but had just a few cows, ponies and chickens. Apparently, local people were paid a gratuity (given a small gift) from the insurance settlement — the size of payment depended upon the nature of the rescue.

Back in Hull, unbeknown to Steve, his wife had a visit from Hellyer's runner. She opened her front-door and was greeted by the blunt words, "Your husband's ship has gone down". Caroline nearly collapsed with shock until the man casually added, "but he's alright".

After three days of taking it easy, a special bus arrived at the farm to collect the shipwrecked crew. They had a bumpy seventy-mile ride over narrow rough track to Reykjavik — capital of Iceland. Fireman Dale remembers the bus journey which wound over the mountains and how they passed the hot-water springs which bubbled in the distance.

Hellyer's port agent, who had arranged the bus, got the crew into the Salvation Army hostel where they either had a room each or shared with another. They were rigged out with clothes and well fed. The hostel was run by a Norwegian couple. Stephen Mahoney struck up a friendly relationship with them. One night the wood-built hostel was nearly sent up in flames. An ex-patient from an over-crowded mental hospital set fire to her bed. Fortunately, the Reykjavik fire-brigade put out the blaze before it spread. It would have been ironic if some of the *Mohican* crew had died in the fire.

The Hull men had to wait while attempts were made by an Icelandic tug, along with the coast-guard vessel *Aegir*, to free their trawler from the Rangar Sands. Reykjavik had no pubs for the Hull men to visit but, with a 'sub' from the agent, they spent time in cafes, sunbathed by a swimming pool, or went to the local picture palace (this was non-smoking, so the men gasped for the break to come). On Sundays, the crew were asked to attend "a bit of a service at the hostel and most went out of respect".

One day, as the men rested, they got an unexpected visitor. An Englishman called Devine came to see them at the hostel after he had read in the local newspaper about their rescue. He was an ex-Sunderland professional footballer who was in Reykjavik to coach an Icelandic club. He asked his fellow Englishmen to form a team to play a friendly match with the locals on their gravel-like pitch. Bill Dale recalls, "as trawlermen we couldn't play for toffee. It was enjoyable though. But that night most of us got severe cramp in our legs".

The seas continued rough for the next couple of weeks. The ceaseless onslaught of the waves drove the *Mohican* further and further along the sands.

*This silhouette shows the **Lord Lloyd** (H.508) rigged out as a war trawler (FY.157) in May 1940. Along with another Hull trawler, **Stella Pegasi** (H.90 – FY.155), they landed British marines who occupied Reykjavik to prevent it falling into German hands. At that time, Iceland was a Danish dependency. When Denmark fell to Hitler's forces, Churchill decided to seize Iceland – crucial to the protection of the Atlantic convoys.*
Courtesy Stephen Mahoney.

*Twenty-three officers and men of H.M.T. **Lord Lloyd**, plus their dog mascot. While the British marines took over Reykjavik, two Hull trawlers took turns to guard the port in case the Germans mounted a counter-invasion. Fortunately for the British, they never did. Stephen Mahoney is on the extreme left, second row from the front. He went to visit the friendly Norwegian couple who ran the Salvation Army Hostel in the port. They were astonished to see him, especially in his smart Royal Navy uniform – much better dressed than just over a year earlier when he was a shipwrecked mariner.*
Courtesy Stephen Mahoney.

Eventually, she broke her back. Trawlerless, the crew were returned to Britain aboard the Icelandic steam ship *Gullfoss*. The men had never had such "lovely meals while afloat" (Hellyers were notorious in that they provided only basic food for their crews). The final leg of their incredible 'fishing trip' was via the *Flying Scotsman* from Leith to Hull. Their families and friends anxiously awaited the men's arrival at Paragon Station. There were no journalists among the small crowd — weeks after the event, there was no news-value in their return home.

When the men reported to Hellyer's ships' husband on dock — lucky to be alive — they were given little regard. Indeed, it was considered 'tough luck' that they had lost all their working gear and personal belongings aboard the *Mohican*. They were forced to buy new gear if they wished to go trawling again. The usual practice was to get rigged out at the owners' Fish Dock store and to have the bill deducted from future settling money. All that Hellyers were prepared to offer the men was another trip. The owners were keen to get them to sea again simply because the men owed the firm money (for 'subs' and clothing in Iceland and debts in Hull). The survivors were given preference when a vacancy occurred on an outward bound trawler. Consequently, the men were sent off on different trawlers such as the *Kurd* (H.344), *Negro* (H.406), *Daneman* (H.37) and the ancient *Earl Kitchener* (H.345 — built in 1915). And so the fourteen *Mohican* crew were all dispersed.

In addition to the material loss of their gear, there was for some a mental cost. At the time of their going aground, there were no obvious problems. Outwardly, they all coped well. It was afterwards that 'reactive nerves' set in. Lofty, for one, became much more aware of the dangers to which his job exposed him. Even going across 'the Pond to Iceland' now seemed full of risks. The shipwreck experience came back to prey on his mind. He was troubled about what might or might not happen: "Was the trawler fishing too close to land?" Before that, "You just took everything for granted", said Stephen, "but afterwards...it wasn't that you lost sleep...but it made you more cautious". On reflection, he summed it up as "a nasty do".

Yet, no matter how gloomy the *Mohican* experience had been, it was soon over-shadowed by the clouds of war. Four months later, in September 1939, most of the Hull trawlermen got their call-up papers and were directed into the Royal Navy Patrol Service.

By a strange twist of fate, Big Steve found himself back in Iceland. He was part of the two-trawler invasion force which landed the marines who took control of Reykjavik (May 1940). The Hull trawlers, *Lord Lloyd* (H.508 — FY.157) and *Stella Pegasi* (H.90 — FY.155), then took it in turns to safeguard the harbour from a German counter-invasion — which never came. While ashore, Steve called into the Salvation Army hostel. The Norwegian couple were surprised and delighted to see him again, especially as he looked so smart in his Royal Navy uniform.

*Two braiders – Mrs. Marrit and Mrs. Hanlon – in Strickland Street around 1912
with a net held over a rail on the terrace wall. They lived in Columbine Terrace
which was owned by the man sitting down. Bill Cody (no doubt nicknamed Buffalo
Bill) watched everyone coming and going in the terrace. If a stranger approached,
he asked their business. His terrace was kept spotless and no-one was allowed to
drop litter.*
Courtesy Ethel Greatwood.

CHAPTER TWELVE

BRAIDING:
NETWORK OF SISTERS

Women braided trawl nets in practically every street of Hull's fishing community. This was especially the case near the Fish Dock between Strickland and Gillett Streets. Rows of women could be seen outside their terraced houses. They chatted away to each other as they handled the twine, needles and spools. The net was hung from a rail, held by two hooks, across the window frame. The older women worked so quickly, "you couldn't see their hands move". In the cold winter months the women braided inside their tiny two-up, two-down 'sham four' houses.

One of these women was Freda Fee whose husband Charlie fixed a couple of hooks either side of the front-room alcove behind the door in their small Boulevard terraced house. She braided while food cooked on the gas stove. After the tea-time meal, she picked up the work again and braided until eleven most nights, and practically all day Sunday. Every Tuesday, like clockwork, Pickering's lorry came to collect the finished nets and left balls of twine to keep her busy during the next week. With the net gone, Freda then set about cleaning her house from top to bottom. The 'terrible dust' from the Manilla hemp got everywhere. She always laid newspapers underneath her coconut mats to collect the dirt.

At Pickering's net loft, Freda's work was carefully measured and recorded. On piece-rates she was only paid for what she did. Every Friday she joined crowds of other braiders to collect her pay. Also in a rush to St. Andrew's Dock, mainly along West Dock Avenue, were the wives of trawlermen at sea going to collect the men's basic weekly wage. This wave of pram-booling women was humorously referred to as the 'Fish Dock Races'.

Freda's mother, Lil Walhelm, worked full-time for Pickering & Haldanes — one of Hull's larger trawling firms. Lil was one of the three Dixon sisters of Walcott Street (Ireland Terrace) who were all braiders at one time or another. As it happened, they were taught to braid by their trawlerman father. The usual pattern, however, was for the mother to teach her daughters the tricks of the trade. A pattern which seems to have emerged is that clusters of sisters braided together. Some of those remembered are: the three Kemp sisters of West Dock Avenue; three girls called Pheasant (born down Walcott Street); three Neal sisters of 52 Witty Street; and the Jessop sisters of Eton Street — it is said that there were six of them, but this has yet to be confirmed.

The demands of the busy trawling industry were so great that many rope firms were also involved in making nets. There were Gourocks at the bottom end of West Dock Avenue (No.106 — see photograph from 1910); the Great Grimsby Coal, Salt & Tannning Co. (COSALT), and Hall's, Barton Ropery —

the last two firms were both on St. Andrew's Dock. Most of my interviews, however, just happened to be with braiders linked with Pickerings. These women worked there before, during and after the Second World War.

Pickerings also had a smallish net-braiding depot on Hessle Road itself. This workshop was in what had been a butcher's shop (Bell's) next door to the bank on the corner of Walcott Street. The dozen or so braiders happily sang old pub songs as they worked such as: *Daisy, Mother Kelly's Doorstep, Nellie Dean,* and the saucy *I Wouldn't Leave My Little Wooden Hut for You.* The friendly atmosphere at the depot was described as "a family affair". The older women helped the young girls — not only with their work, but also with personal problems to do with boyfriends or family squabbles. Young braiders usually had been taught by their mothers, but when they joined Pickering's workshop each girl had to complete a fortnight's training. By and large, this was as a 'needle filler' who kept about six braiders supplied. She was paid out of the braiders' wages, not by the company.

The ten-inch, flat wooden needle, about an inch across, was usually held in the right hand. The rough twine was looped inside the pointed needle on to a lug and pulled very tightly by the left hand. During this rapid motion, the girls pressed against their left hip to get a firm grip. As a result, a hole was soon worn on that side of their apron. Some older women hung a piece of leather from a belt to protect their clothes.

The girls got tiny spells (splinters) in their fingers from the coarse sisal twine. Soft hands soon blistered — a problem which put off the less hardy. One tip to toughen the skin was to soak both hands in methylated spirits every night —"failing that, we were told to use the piss-pot". The tough twine also made the girls' hands bleed. The skin cracked along the edge, especially the little fingers. Their hands often looked a mess and were sometimes covered with sticking plasters. Freda Fee had hard skin across her palms. She said, "I never had lady's hands...I used to hide them in company so that no-one could see the callouses". A more serious longer-term problem was arthritic hands.

The young novice had to buy her own set of needles, at least four dozen (but once established, some braiders had around two hundred on the go). The main Hull supplier of wooden needles and spools was Tom Capes who made them in his back-yard shed on a machine. He lived at No.40 West Dock Avenue (he took over the business begun in the same house by his father John in 1900). The needles cost 2/- (10p) per dozen. The helpful Mrs. Capes dealt with the girls' orders.They waited on the door-step while she got what they wanted.

An older woman once played a joke on a new needle-filler. She got some herring from the fish-house, hid them in a net and kidded the youngster that they had just been caught. Another source of amusement was "Olive's false-teeth". The Hessle Road workshop was in a converted house and there was a sink in what had been a back bedroom. Olive often got a good wash there, but sometimes unknowingly left her dentures on the mantle-piece for all to see.

Another trial for any new girl was to ask her to pull an old net out of store. Large black cockroaches scurried out all over the place — "real big things". Some women ran away scared, while others laughingly chased after the beetles and delighted in the sound of the crack as they stamped on them. If a new girl

The Gourock Ropework Company was one of a handful of firms who made trawl nets. These twelve braiders are outside the West Dock Avenue depot at "the tunnel end" – which meant near the entrance, under the railway lines, to St.Andrew's Dock. The young girl in black on the front row is Jenny Young (née Robinson) of Eton Street. This picture was taken in 1910 – at the same time her sister Esther was away from Hull as a herring girl (see Chapter 4).
Courtesy Stanley Young.

Lil Walhelm is a heroine of the Second World War. Like many women, however, her home-front deeds have been ignored. This is her pass which permitted her access to the St.Andrew's Fish Dock. From there, she organised the production of camouflage netting by 1500 braiders throughout the port. Despite a fear of the telephone, and the frequent night-time air-raids, she and her sister Ada Dixon kept output high.
Courtesy Freda Fee.

A fair number of sisters braided together in the fishing community. Above are the Sayer sisters of Gillett Street: Maud Morgan and Doris Leyden (c.1933). Braiding in the terrace meant that a mother could be at home when her children returned from school. The work gave the women some extra money for the family, and was also a chance for them to chat.
Courtesy Rose Clark.

lasted the two weeks, she had a trade: "you had to be taught braiding and once you learned, you never forgot how to do it".

Braiders often took home a hessian bag with balls of twine and needles to fill in the evening "to get a good start the next day". Some girls even 'roped' in their boyfriends to help with this work. Young locomotive fireman Arthur Chambers did this for Marian Wilson in their courting days. Many of the young lasses had boyfriends on the trawlers. When the trawlerlads were in port between trips, with lots of settling money to spend, they gathered outside the workshop. They shouted up to the girls, who then leaned out of the first floor windows. A length of twine was lowered to which the lads tied a packet of cigarettes for the girls' break-time smoke. The forewoman got annoyed when she saw a box of cigs dangle up past the ground floor window.

The work itself involved the production of a 150-foot trawl net which had five main sections. The difficulty of the piece determined the rate of pay. The 'square' was the large top part of the trawl and could take over a week to complete (the post-WWII pay was £3/15/0d — 375p. per piece). There was also the baiting or belly (underneath), a pair of wings (for each side), and the cod-end. This was the most difficult part to make (the finer mesh was braided with smaller needles and spools).

A number of the older braiders were married to trawlermen. Pickerings, being trawler owners, appreciated the domestic demands on a woman during her husband's brief stay at home after three weeks away. Therefore, if a wife did not come into work, "everyone knew that her net would not be in that week while her man was home". There is a story of a pregnant braider, about to have her first child, who rushed to finish a net so her mother could get it to the dock before 5 pm. The poor woman gave birth not long after at half-past-five.

The Second World War upset the regular patterns in the Hessle Road community. Most of the trawlermen went off to serve in "Harry Tate's Navy" (the Royal Navy Patrol Service) — many aboard converted Hull fishing vessels. Meanwhile, the braiders were also employed in the war effort. Their nets were ideal camouflage for the front-line forces to conceal tanks and equipment from the enemy.

The switch from peace- to war-time braiding was not overnight. With the outbreak of war, practically all the women were stood off and forced to find other employment such as shopwork, at the Cod Liver Oil factory on Hedon Road, or doing heavy work on the railways. Others joined the forces, and some decided to get married and stay home. The drastically reduced Hull fishing fleet had more than enough surplus nets to keep the few trawlers amply supplied with gear, so the women's services were not needed.

Then suddenly, "in 1940," "they sent for us to do the nets". The War Department contracted Pickerings to supply them with camouflage. Lil Walhelm, was put in charge of the braiders to produce nets to War Department specifications.

Camouflage pieces were not as big as the trawl nets. They were made by braiding a diamond-shaped net. That is, the women began with one loop, added two to that, then four on the next row, and doubled the number with each row. At a pre-set half-way point, the process was reversed until one loop

The war-time braiders are making camouflage nets down Somerset Street in a depot known as "Roys" above a cobbler's shop (c.1941). This small room looked packed with women. At least ten depots were scattered in various buildings all around Hull. The working atmosphere was friendly and patriotic songs were sung throughout the working day.
Courtesy Lily Rylett.

Seven Lord Line braiders on the flat roof of the St.Andrew's Fish Dock building in the 1950s. They represent all ages, with two young novice braiders at the front. Their apprenticeship as a needle-filler soon determined whether or not they could stick at the braiding craft. It was essential that they could "take a joke" and fit in with the older women. It was also hard on their soft school-girl hands as their skin blistered from the rough twine.
Courtesy Marion Chambers.

Twenty-eight braiders gather on the top floor of the Lord Line buildings to wish Lil Walhelm a happy retirement in August 1956. They bought her a shopping bag, fruit, sweets and flowers. She was a well-loved forewoman who engendered a wholesome family atmosphere among the women who worked under her. Even after Lil left the firm, she continued to braid at home until she was moved to Orchard Park Estate. Courtesy Marion Chambers.

was again reached. Forewoman Annie Davies (later Mrs. Derbyshire) checked each braider's net with a yard-stick. She knew instantly if one loop had been missed out. When a fault was found the braider was sent over to work on Annie's net while she put right the mistake. She was a "fair forewoman who did all the measuring".

After a piece had been checked, the next stage was called 'scrimming'. A three-inch strip of hessian was woven in and out of the mesh. This dirty brown and green material produced the camouflage-effect. The work was carried out with the net hung on a large beam. "By the time we got home, we used to be all the colours of the rainbow from the dyed hessian." The piece of camouflage was laid out flat on the floor and two women then folded, rolled, and fastened up the bundle with string, ready for transport to the war front.

The demands of war soon increased the need for more camouflage and soon Lil ended up in charge of 1500 braiders who were scattered throughout the city in ten depots, with St. Andrew's Dock as the main centre. The key places on the dock were in Pickerings own net-loft at the eastern end of the dock; the Ice House building "it was a hell of a big place with hundreds of women there"; and on the old Cod Farm. Freda Fee recalls how "a lorry took about twenty of us beyond the slip [where trawlers were repaired] to an old empty fish house. There were big rats running about. Someone would shout, 'Oh! Look! There's a rat!' and the women started to scream."

Other depots in Hull (used at different times) were at Bean Street; Roy's along Somerset Street (both off Hessle Road); in Craft's, the former posh Hessle Road department store, which had been empty for years; some premises near the King Billy statue in the Market Place; a warehouse at Blundell's Corner along the Spring Bank side; and an empty garage on Princes Avenue. In addition to the production at these various depots, there were women who still worked at home in the Hessle Road fishing community whose braided nets also fed into the system.

It was a complex operation which needed a vast amount of careful co-ordination. Lil did this despite her fear of the telephone. She was 'a bag of nerves' when she had to answer a call and so used to shout very loud. Her voice could be heard from over the other side of the busy, noisy net loft. But she and her sister Ada were both considered 'good scholars' whose records and book-keeping were very detailed.

The women were a loyal workforce who sang patriotic songs as they worked. One woman would start and everybody joined in with songs like: *We'll Meet Again, White Cliffs of Dover, Lilly Marlene, Pack Up Your Troubles in Your Old Kit Bag, It's a Long Way to Tipperary*. The women had some good laughs: 'everyone was jolly...never heard no grumbling...and we did not realise the dangers of war, except when the planes came over".

The heavy and regular night-time raids which Hull suffered often played havoc with the camouflage production. The policy of having depots spread all over the city perhaps contained a hidden logic; if one was bombed, then output could continue elsewhere. The main Pickering building was badly bombed during a particularly concentrated attack targeted at the Fish Dock. Next morning, the braiders found only a pile of smouldering rubble. They were told to go home; but with no work, there was no pay. Eventually, the braiders were dispersed into other jobs until the end of the war.

In the early 1950's Pickerings (then re-named Lord Line) opened a large re-constructed building near the entrance to St. Andrew's Dock — on the same site as the one bombed in the war. The large top-floor area was used as a net loft where men were employed to fix the various sections of net together into a complete trawl ready for deep-sea fishing.

The braiders from the homely Hessle Road depot were transferred into this new building. The women, however, soon made the new place their own. Friday afternoons were usually a slack period for the braiders — a perfect time to enjoy the 'Fish Dock Races'. The Lord Line women looked out for their friends — some were former workmates. They eyed up the wives' fashions to see who was 'going up in the world' and who had bought what from The Clothing House on Hessle Road. At Christmas they decorated the loft with trimmings and a tree.

Lord Line was the first Hull firm to install a Baader net-making machine from Germany. But they and other trawl-makers did not move into mechanization out of choice. It was forced upon them by a change in the attitude of the women they employed. Or, to be more precise, the lack of younger women who wanted to be employed as braiders.

This labour shortage situation is well outlined on the front-page article of the *Hull & Yorkshire Times* (12th May 1962). In the early 1960s, youngsters no longer needed to do the hard braiding work for such low pay as their mothers had done. The girls looked around and saw that they could get easier jobs (in factories, shops, or offices) for better wages and without the penny-pinching apprenticeship of a needle-filler. So it was the younger women who turned their backs on the trawling industry's poor pay and conditions, and thereby forced them to bring in more expensive technology.

Initially, the machines could only do straight strips of net and, temporarily, created a few extra jobs while 'teething problems' were sorted out (and more sophisticated models were devised). The more complicated pieces were still braided by the older women. Even the trawler owners admitted that the hand-made nets were of a much better quality than those produced on the early machinery.

Gradually, improved equipment was introduced and nylon replaced the hemp twine. Eventually, the small band of older-generation braiders were no longer needed. Their old craft and skills faded out. Some would say, "That's progress". But no amount of technology can ever replace the good-hearted warmth and joy spun by the women net-braiders of Hessle Road.

*Hull trawler **Warwick Deeping** (H.136), armed as a war trawler (FY.182). She sank
in the English Channel on 12th October 1940 after being hunted down by five
German destroyers. This picture was taken earlier that year in the Bristol Channel
where a giant French submarine was sighted by the crew. The **Deeping** escorted the
tug and sub into Swansea.
Courtesy Jim Fuller.*

CHAPTER THIRTEEN

WARWICK DEEPING:
WAR TRAWLER

In the Second World War, Hull lost a total of one-hundred trawlers. Eighty-one of these were destroyed while in Admiralty Service. Twenty-six were sunk during air attacks, nineteen by mines, ten by surface warships, eight by submarine, and eighteen as a result of various other causes. The ten sunk by warships, in alphabetical order (with their former Hull registration number), were: *Adonis* (ex. *Nordav I* — H.308), *Argyllshire* (H.145), *Avanturine* (H.197), *Cayton Wyke* (H.440), *Jasper* (ex. *Balthasar* — H.405), *Lord Hailsham* (H.82), *Lord Stonehaven* (H.103), *Pelton* (H.228), *Stella Dorado* (ex. *Cape Teriberski* — H.168), and *Warwick Deeping* (H.136). Most of these losses took place during German E-boat attacks. This chapter highlights the noble *Warwick Deeping*. This former Hull trawler was pursued and sunk by five German destroyers. Despite a heavy pounding, she kept afloat long enough for all her crew to escape with their lives.

The *Warwick Deeping* story began in October 1940 when Britain was braced for invasion by the triumphant troops of Hitler's Third Reich. British Intelligence knew of the German *Operation Sea Lion* plans to invade. Every Admiralty vessel was fully deployed, especially the 550-ton anti-submarine converted trawler (FY.182),

Very low on food and fuel H.M.T. *Warwick Deeping* put into Portsmouth for supplies. The provisions had only just been loaded when the trawler got an emergency call. The message was so urgent there was no time to wait for a couple of the crew who had gone ashore, or to get over to the hoists to fill up with coal. When the ship put to sea again "she was like a balloon" high afloat out of the water — a blessing in disguise, as it happened. Later that evening, the *Warwick Deeping* was on duty in the English Channel with H.M.T. *L'istrac* as part of the anti-invasion patrol.

The two trawlers were spotted by a pack of hit-and-run German destroyers. The five craft, *Wolf, Falke, Grief, Kondor,* and *Seeadler,* pelted toward the trawlers at the top-notch speed of 21-knots. They were under the command of a Captain Henne. His orders were simple — attack any British shipping in the Channel to cause havoc. In this encounter, at 2327 hours, 11th October, there was confusion and mistakes on both sides. The Germans mistook the trawlers for two British coasters; while the trawler crews initially believed that the on-coming Germans were Royal Navy vessels.

The first salvos were directed toward the *Warwick Deeping*. In the panic, and still under the illusion that the destroyers were British, the 778-ton *L'istrac* switched on her identification lights. The German gunners could not believe their luck. Suddenly they had an easy target and took full advantage of it. The

When the Second World War was declared all the Hull trawlermen in the Royal Navy Reserve (RNR) got their orders to report immediately to the Patrol Service HQ at Lowestoft. The base there was affectionately named Sparrow's Nest (after a Theatre on the site). These two prints are of the men (1940) and officers (1943) who trained there before being dispersed to naval bases all over the world. In Portsmouth, youngsters used to joke about the "R.N.R." abbreviations. They shouted to the men that they stood for "Really Not Required" – a view very far from the truth.
Courtesy Jim Fuller.

*Fortunately, some of the equipment from the H.M.T. **Warwick Deeping** (FY.182) has been brought up from the bottom of the English Channel and is on display to the public. Diver and marine historian Martin Woodward has these (and numerous other shipwreck items) featured in his six-gallery Maritime Museum at Bembridge, Isle of Wight. From the **Deeping** is the ship's bell, gun range-finder, and the large compass binnacle from the ASDIC (Anti-Submarine Detection) deck – shown above. Copyright Martin Woodward.*

old 1907 trawler received the full brunt of the German thunder. Shells smashed into her boiler room, there was a large explosion and, as she began to sink, the *Grief* finished her off with a torpedo. The *L'istrac* was blown apart and "the flames of hell lit the mid-night sky".

The crewmen of the vulnerable *Warwick Deeping* were now in a hopeless position. The Germans lost no time and fired a series of torpedoes at the 156-foot trawler. Some official RN records claim that the *Warwick Deeping* was sunk by torpedo. This is not true. Instead, the deadly explosives passed 'harmlessly' beneath the trawler because she was so high out of the water. Had the coal been loaded, she would have been blown to smithereens and finished off in no time. The sea gods were on her side, for a while longer at least.

Acting Leading Seaman Jim Fuller, and another rating, decided there was little they could do on the ASDIC (submarine-detection) deck. They sprang down from above the bridge to find the trawler aimlessly adrift. Jim took the wheel. Immediately, he rang double full ahead to George the chief engineer — a fellow Hull trawlerman. He got the ship going straight away and Jim steered desperately toward England.

Predators *Falke* and *Kondor* went in hot pursuit of the *Warwick Deeping*. As their torpedoes 'strangely' missed, they began heavy shell-fire. The first volley hit the bow close to the 4.7″ gun — just before the gunnery officer had time to man his station. Meanwhile, the secret code books (specially weighted with lead) were removed from the ship's safe and dumped overboard. Jim anxiously steered a zig-zag course to make the trawler a difficult target to hit. Even so, the ship took several blows. When the engine-room was struck, the trawler began to take water. With the *L'istrac* gone, everyone firmly believed the *Warwick Deeping* would soon follow.

After he mumbled a few silent prayers, the terror suddenly left Jim and he became calm. Each time he altered course (two points either side of north), he could hear and feel the water swill about inside the ship. As the tension increased, Jim began to plead with the *Warwick Deeping*, "Come on old girl, please keep going". She seemed to understand. After a tremble and shudder, she slowly struggled upright each time.

Jim had a deep bond of love and affection for this 'old girl' from his home port. He had begun his war days aboard her in the Bristol Channel. At that time, she had been on guard patrol just west of Lundy Island. One day Jim had spotted a huge red submarine on the horizon. It was so big it looked more like an enormous air-craft carrier as it got nearer to the *Warwick Deeping*. The crew were even more amazed when they realised it was being towed by a tiny tug. *La Creole*, had been taken brand new from a French shipyard by the tug crew to prevent her being seized by the advancing Germans. The *Deeping* escorted the tug and sub into Swansea. It is believed to have stayed there awhile, was perhaps damaged by shrapnel during a German air-raid, but later put into service by the Royal Navy.

Now, in the heat of battle in the English Channel, Jim was about to end his links with the *Warwick Deeping*. The barrage continued, the wheelhouse windows were smashed, a piece of glass just missed Jim's eye and cut his forehead; otherwise, he was alright. Jim was reluctant to see her die easily and

As in the First World War (see Chapter 3), the Second ended with celebrations and peace-parties all over Britain. Churches rang their bells for the first time in years and ships blasted their hooters. There were countless street parties. This post-war party was inside Scarborough Street School for the children of the area.
Courtesy Ethel Warcup.

his heart ached with every roll as she took longer and longer to come back on an even keel. Inevitably, the engines slowly ground to a halt. The battling engineer called up the voice-pipe that the water was at a dangerous level. The *Warwick Deeping* laid over to port as she slowly filled.

And then, "miracle of miracles", the Germans gradually eased and then ceased their fire. In the quiet calm that followed, Grimsby ASDIC-man Len Smith said, "Thank God" as he stuck a cig in Jim's mouth and praised him for his swift action to effect their escape. The order was given to abandon ship.

As Jim clambered over the side, to join the others in the lifeboat he patted the rail of the *Warwick Deeping* and tearfully said "Well done old girl, and thanks". Remarkably, not one of the 22-man crew had been killed. The lifeboat could not hold all the men, so some hung onto Carley Floats (cork rings) which were lashed together and towed behind the boat. They rowed north and left the *Warwick Deeping* as she slowly sank.

In all their chaos they believed they were twenty miles south of the English coast. Recent evidence, however, has proved the *Warwick Deeping* was much nearer than they imagined. Marine historian and deep-sea diver Martin Woodward has located the wreck of this Hull trawler just five miles south of the Isle of Wight. Items from this warship are now displayed at his Maritime Museum in Bembridge (IoW). But, back in the cold October of 1940 as the vessel plunged to the seabed, its survivors found themselves alone in the pitch dark. The bedraggled crew had no light except a morse lamp. After an hour or so, a small fishing coble picked up their signal, got a line to the boat, towed them to the Isle of Wight, and left them somewhere on the coast.

After being turned away from a big posh house by a haughty couple, the damp and chilled warriors eventually got a warm welcome — at three o'clock in the morning — from a friendly pub landlord and his wife. They generously put bottles of spirits on the bar and invited the brave seafarers to help themselves. Within no time, the whole crew of the *Warwick Deeping* were merrily singing their heads off as if nothing had happened.

CHAPTER FOURTEEN

DILLINGER:
DARE-DEVIL

There are countless yarns about Hessle Road's Dillinger. He clowned about so much he was like a one-man circus. Yet, like most funny performers, his jokes hid a tear. Dillinger was a man of extremes. From the well of deep despair he sprang into a world of frenzied fun. Once in that state, he vowed to remain there "at all costs". Everything he did, he did for laughs — regardless of what others thought.

People either liked or disliked Dillinger; but no-one could overlook him. In drawing together some of his varied and fantastic escapades, it is hard to decide if Dillinger was a joker or hero. Some were afraid of his outlandish behaviour, while others admired him as a rebellious comedian. Many, however, commented on his "warm nature". No matter what, he was a dynamic character who fully deserves a place in the history of the community. He is one of its legendary figures. Indeed, Ron Haines, a wireless operator who sailed with him, stated, "They ought to build a statue to Dillinger".

'Dillinger' was his nickname, of course. He was christened Walter Denton. Information about his parents is a bit sketchy, but they were both Hull people who lived off Hessle Road, along Westbourne Street (9 Marlbro' Terrace). Their names were Arthur and Mary 'Lizzie' Elizabeth (née Bilton). They both worked in the fishing industry as fish-house workers. Arthur also did a bit of bobbing, while Lizzie sometimes travelled around the country with her mother as a herring girl. The two women followed the Scottish herring drifters around the coast (in a similar way to the women described in Chapter Four). Lizzie was a strong Roman Catholic with some Irish blood in her (while Arthur was probably Protestant, if anything). Married around 1912, their first boy was named Arthur after his dad.

Walter was born in the middle of the First World War (8th September 1916) in Burntisland, near Kirkcaldy. Lizzie's father was a chief engineer based in Fife with the Royal Navy. While her husband Arthur served abroad, pregnant Lizzie joined her parents in Scotland well away from the Zeppelin raids over Hull. After the war, the Denton family settled back again in Hull's fishing community. Walter later followed his older brother into St.Wilfrid's Roman Catholic School in the Boulevard. [The Dentons had two more children: Maria (1921) and Christopher (1923) — he died when only five years old, but little is known about the girl].

Walter's life-long friend, Harold Petrini, remembers their days at St. Wilfrid's School. One of his stories shows how Walter was a bit of a tearaway even as a young boy. He always carried a catapult in his back-pocket. One day, as the teacher chalked on the black-board, Walt fired an ink-soaked paper

Twelve-year old Walter Denton with his Aunt Lizzie Preston. She lived at No.1 St. Andrew's Terrace, Gillett Street where Walt stayed most weekends. Next door was the Petrini family, whose son Harold was Walt's best mate. They played together over the weekend. They were also in the same class at St.Wilfrid's Roman Catholic School on the Boulevard.
Courtesy Arthur Denton.

*Dillinger (left) in 1936 with a gangster-like trilby to suit his tough-guy nickname. With him is his close friend Jimmy Portz who was lost aboard the **Admiral Collingwood** (H.341) in December that year. A gloomy time for Walter because his older brother Arthur was lost in the same shipwreck.*
Courtesy Arthur Denton.

pellet at the back of her head. He then quickly handed his weapon to Potts, the lad next to him. The teacher angrily walked up to Potts, grabbed the catapult, and clouted him hard on the back of his head. Walter left school around 1931 to find work in Hull's fishing industry.

Yet how was it that Walter Denton got nicknamed after U.S. Public Enemy No.1? Killer John Dillinger hit the headlines worldwide in 1933 with daring bank robberies and bold escapes from the law. A year later, the F.B.I. ambushed and gunned him down outside a Chicago cinema. Young Walter Denton was anointed with this villainous title when he was a 17-year old trawlerlad. But, as with any larger-than-life character, there is more than one story about the same event. The most popular is the trawler 'fish room' story. As a group of deckhands chopped ice, one of them jibed that Denton was a "Lazy b.....d". In a hot-headed impulse, Walt swung his large mallet at the name-caller. The man was out for the count. Onlookers were silently aghast until the fishroom man cried out, "Who the hell do you think you are? You're worse than John Dillinger".

Another version is told by Harold Petrini who often sailed with his friend Walter. His account is more specific, colourful, and in tune with Denton's playful nature. They were both young trawlerlads aboard the *Imperialist* (H.2) with the famous Snowy Worthington — Hellyer's top skipper. Unbeknown to everyone, Walter sneaked aboard a box of fireworks to have his own Guy Fawkes fun on 5th November 1934. While on early watch he secretly placed a line of crackers on deck, fastened by a piece of twine. The first haul was heaved aboard at day-break. It was the mates precarious job to get underneath the heavy bag to untie the cod-end and release the tons of fish onto the deck. Secretly, Walter put a match to the first firework to set off the BANG, BANG, BANG, one after another. The mate was shocked and furious. He pointed at young Denton and said, "You're worse than Dillinger!" And so the name stuck for the rest of his life (and beyond).

This hard-man image and reputation probably made Walter more daring than he might otherwise have been. He was fairly well-built and this was maybe another reason why he got away with his madcap antics. Walt enjoyed his infamous nickname and even took to wearing a Dillinger-style gangster trilby (see photograph).

Three years later, the man of fun was struck by pain. In 1937, grief piled upon grief for Walter. No sooner had the New Year begun when grave doubts centred around the whereabouts of the Hull trawler *Admiral Collingwood* (H.341). Among the eighteen-man crew of this three-month old vessel was not only Walt's married brother Arthur, whom he looked up to, but his close friend Jimmy Portz from Rugby Street (Fern Grove). On the return from a Christmas fishing trip off Bear Island, the 448-ton super-trawler ran into a severe hurricane and was driven ashore at Ona Island on the west coast of Norway, near Alesund. The whole crew perished. The ship was never traced except for pieces of wreckage scattered along the rocky coast.

Before young twenty-year old Walter had time to come to terms with this double loss he was given an even greater emotional blow. His beloved mother died. Lizzie's cancerous condition worsened after the loss of her oldest boy

Arthur aboard the *Collingwood*. She was only forty-seven years old. In the blackest grief Walter stood by his mother's grave and helplessly sobbed his heart out. It is believed that this was the turning point in his life. Relatives recall that he said to his father, "There you are, that's the first time you've ever seen me cry and it'll be the last. Nobody is ever going to see me shed another tear".

From that day forth, Walt buried his agony beneath a mountain of laughter and jokes. If ever he felt depressed it was soon drowned out by drink. Within a year, his father died, That left Walter the sole survivor of the Denton family. He went to live with Aunt Charlotte. With no immediate family to bridle him, bachelor Dillinger began his wild horseplay.

Horses, indeed, featured in a number of the Dillinger stories. He once drove underneath a horse on a motor-bike. Another time, on the 'dry side' of St. Andrew's Fish Dock, he came across an unattended horse and cart. It belonged to Chrissie Wilkie (Christopher Wilkinson), a bag-collector who removed the crewmen's heavy work clothes when they were finished from a trawler. Chrissie had an artificial hand (from a WWII injury during the invasion of Italy) and so it took him a while to clamber from ship to ship, sometimes three or more deep on the southside of the dock. While Chrissie was away, Dillinger unshackled 'Peggy', placed the shafts between some nearby railings and then harnessed her back into them. He did not stop there. From the cart he took two pairs of sea boots to fit onto her hooves and a sou'wester hat which he fastened upon Peggy's head. Dill and Petrini then dashed over the swing bridge and hid near the Tideman's Office to watch what happened. Chrissie got the surprise of his life when he saw his horse and cart in an impossible position. The two men began to laugh out loud. Chrissie looked around and shouted across the lockpit, "You Dillinger! I might have known it was you!"

Another equine tale tells of the time when Dillinger rode into Rayners pub on a pony and caused an uproar. On a different occasion in Rayners (c.1938), a group of bobbers were having a game of dominoes when one of them remarked about the noisy racket from the horses hooves in West Dock Avenue. Dillinger dashed outside where he tied sacking around the feet of a scrap-merchant's horse to muffle the sound. Race horses were also a pre-occupation: "Dill loved to bet". A gambling spirit is certainly in line with his risk-taking character. No doubt, many of the illegal 'cowboy bookies' of Hessle Road knew him well.

Rayners, 'the fishermen's pub', has already been mentioned and, with it being near his Harrow Street home, Dillinger spent lots of shore-time there. Dill was one of 'The Three Musketeers' along with his mates 'Pat' Petrini and 'Jimmy Mac' (Jim MacCarthy). Dill was so close to these friends that their names were tattooed on his back under the heading "My Friends" (a third name was that of Jimmy Portz who disappeared with the loss of the *Admiral Collingwood*). Whenever the three landed in Hull together, "we had a ding-dong". Other drinking-mates in the gang, most with nicknames, were: 'Skedge' (skipper Hardy), 'Bunny' Ebden, 'Jay-Jay' (Jack Downes), Freddie Fall, Chris Charleton, Freddie Cassie, and 'Lighthouse' (a tall thin man). A regular practice of Dill's, when it was his turn to buy a round of beer, was to roll a pound note into a ball between the palms of his hands, sling it to the barman and shout out loudly, "Get some more slurp over here". The air was usually

"You can always tell a trawlerman ashore" is a frequent Hessle Road expression. The men took a great deal of pride in their appearance. Dillinger and his mates were no exception. They wore smart made-to-measure suits and had neatly-trimmed hair. Trilby-wearing Dill poses in Jerome's Studio along Whitefriargate (8th November 1938).
Courtesy Arthur Denton.

Many trawlermen got their suits made at Waistell's, directly across from the fishermen's pub – Rayners. After the three o'clock closing-time crewmen, with pockets full of settling money, went to collect a suit ordered before they sailed. And, while in the tailor's shop, got measured for another.
Courtesy Len Pearson.

When the pubs threw out, some trawlermen went straight into a social club.
Dillinger was a member of the St.Andrew's Social Club in West Dock Avenue (and
no doubt others too). This photo in the club shows him with a tattoo on his right
hand. Some of his other tattoos were a heart with the words "MOTHER", and on
the fingers of each hand the letters "L-O-V-E" and "H-A-T-E".
Courtesy Arthur Denton.

blue with foul language. Most Hull trawlermen moderated their language in the presence of a woman. But not Dillinger. It made no difference to him if it was mixed company or not.

After one drinking bout in Rayners, Dillinger stacked a pile of about sixteen empty pint glasses, one inside the other, on the floor. Everyone looked on in the noisy room as he shouted over to the landlord, "How much is this lot worth?" When told their value, he then picked up a heavy stone ash-tray from the table, placed it on top of the pile and pressed down hard. The glasses shattered. He stepped over the broken glass, went up to the bar, paid for the damage, and asked for a brush and shovel to sweep up the mess.

Not surprisingly, Dillinger got banned from the premises from time to time. His response was simply to take his custom across West Dock Avenue to St. Andrew's Social Club. In his wake came about twenty drinking mates. The story goes that the landlord of Rayners then asked him to return (and, no doubt, bring the other customers back too). Dill only agreed if he was given a drink 'on the house'.

Dillinger liked to send-up those in authority. Not only did he challenge landlords ashore, but also skippers afloat. Two trawling tales tell how he conned worried skippers to give him a few swigs of whisky. Walt knew that countless crewmen had lost fingers when the trawl gear was hauled aboard. So, on one trip, he gave out a horrendous screech as the two-ton trawl door crashed against the side of the ship. He gripped his left hand as he doubled over in agony. Everyone feared his fingers were crushed. They took him up to the wheel-house. The skipper pleaded with him to take off the mitten so the injury could be treated. Dillinger refused, but his stance softened with a few gulps of liquor. After the third dram was swallowed, he pulled out his hand, wriggled his fingers and said, "Thanks skipper, that's much better now".

The same wheeze worked a few years later with a different skipper aboard another trawler. This time his buffoonery was more extreme and gory. As he gutted a live coley, a fish with a large heart, he cut out the organ and covertly put it in his mouth. He then mimicked an epileptic fit as he spat blood out all over himself and the deck. Predictably, anxious crewmen carried him up to the skipper and Dill got his alcoholic reward — which he probably deserved for his melodramatics. Perhaps it should be said that the average three-week trip to the Arctic fishing grounds was fairly routine, and monotonous; so at least Dillinger's skylarking broke the boredom and gave the crew a laugh.

The Second World War was declared (3rd September, 1939) just five days before Walter's twenty-third birthday. He rarely spoke about his war-time experience, but willingly joined his fellow trawlermen in Britain's naval battle with Germany. In step with his devil-may-care nature, he volunteered for the perilous ball-bearing runs to Sweden. These were operated by Ellerman's Wilson Line from Hull's Albert Dock, under the Red Ensign, on behalf of the Ministry of War Transport. These moon-less night missions were dangerous. In rapid 48-ton MGBs (motor gun boats), they sped from Hull to Lysekil, near Gothenborg to get the much-needed SKF bearings to keep the British war machines in action. The crews were selected for their "venturous spirit and reliability". The 1000-mile trips took place mainly in the winter months of 1943-44.

The official name of Rayners pub was originally "Star & Garter" – but the Hessle Roaders never called it that. Dillinger's Harrow Street home (No.41) was not far away from the fishermen's pub. At one time his drinking mates were inside awaiting Dill's arrival when the door burst open. Over his shoulder was a thick mooring rope at which he tugged, strained and cursed, "Come on you b.....d!" Everyone looked on and expected a large animal or object to appear; but in came a tiny three-week old puppy dog.
Copyright Alec Gill.

Dillinger in Rayners. His broad grin reflects the joyous nature he had toward life. He once rode on a pony into this public-house. Generally, his wild antics were good-humoured, harmless, and intended to inject fun into the repetitive workaday routine ashore and afloat. Like most Hull trawlermen, he was very generous. But in Dill's case "he was silly with his money too... He'd never lend you money, he'd rather give it to you".
Courtesy Arthur Denton.

Sailor Denton did about two or three trips to Sweden in the fast gunboats. The rest of his war service was aboard converted trawlers (probably mine-sweeping and convoy escort work). Twice he had to abandon ship after being under attack. During one of these, all the crew were safely in the life-boat when one of them exclaimed that he had left his gold wedding ring in his cabin. As the converted trawler had not yet gone down, Dillinger (being a very strong swimmer) slipped over the side and swam off to the half-submerged warship. Sometime later, Dill arrived back at the life-boat and gave the ring to an astonished sailor. Also in his pocket was a bottle of rum which, he joked, was the main reason he risked his life going to the trawler — it also kept him warm in the cold water.

In 1940, Walter married recently-widowed Sarah Nelson who had lost her first husband in the early months of the war (killed in action aboard a mine-sweeper in the English Channel and decorated posthumously). The two met through Walt's Aunt Charlotte who was a friend of Sarah. The Dentons got an extra food ration because of the Swedish ball-bearing work (on top of his danger money). Among this was tinned fruit — a rarity during the shortages of war. He threw the empty cans into the street to show off that his family had such a luxury.

One of the best-known pranks in the Dillinger catalogue also took place during WWII. This was when he switched babies between prams. Some accounts say this was outside Woollies on Hessle Road, but the event actually took place at Bevin House, George Street, near North Bridge. It was a bright summer's day and inside the building dozens of mothers queued for their ration of (or coupons for) special baby food (National Dried Milk). Dillinger and Petrini had just left Bevin House when Dill noticed a little coloured boy in a shabby pram. He immediately took pity and decided to switch him with a child from a posh-looking pram. Dill did not stop there. Before the two men left the scene, other babies were swapped over. "There was hell on, and some mothers screamed out in anguish". The police were called, but had no idea who did it. Hopefully, it was all sorted out in the end and each mother went home with her own child!

Come VE-Day (8th May, 1945) Dillinger, along with millions of others throughout Europe, went berserk. He was driven about by his regular driver — George Lee — in his open-top, hearse-like taxi. The town centre was packed with revellers. Everyone was in a jubilant state and, as Dill's taxi passed a policeman on point duty, he stuck a bottle of beer in the officer's out-stretched hand as the cab sped by.

There is an interesting post-war story told about Dillinger by ex-bobber (and now town-market fish retailer) 'Smokey Joe'. He recalls how demobbed Dillinger and other ex-servicemen went to find work on St.Andrew's Fish Dock. They obviously needed new gear (oil skins, gutting knives, etc.) to go Arctic trawling again. Dillinger leapt over the broad oak-topped counter of the trawler owners' fish dock store (at the corner of 'Tobacco Road'), grabbed clothes from the shelves, tossed them over to his mates and said, "There you are lads! We shouldn't have to pay for these now".

Being married and a parent seemed to make no difference to Walter's high level of tom-foolery. Sarah Denton was at home late one evening when there was a knock at their unlocked door. She assumed, from previous nights that it was taxi-driver George who had brought Walt home dead drunk, so simply called out, "Sling him in the passage". The reply came back, "We can't, he's in an ambulance with a broken leg". It seems that he tempted providence a bit too much that evening and his ploy, whatever it was, had not come off.

Dillinger's audacious tricks at sea continued unchecked as he clowned about even more. The *Othello* (H.581) — Hull's last coal-burner — trawled up a WWII mine in 1952 (not an unusual event during those post-war trips). Walter was aboard with his 10-year old son, Arthur, who was on a 'pleasure' trip. After the frightful mine hit the deck, Dillinger grabbed a hammer and pretended to bash away at one of its spikes. Complete pandemonium broke out as crewmen pleaded with him to stop.

Although Walt was essentially a trawlerman, he sometimes went 'big boating'. That is, got work as an A.B. (able-bodied seaman) on the larger cargo ships of the merchant fleet. Perhaps he had to do this after his Arctic antics in order to give the fishing fraternity time to cool down. Fate drew Dillinger back into trawling in 1964.

Just before Christmas that year, Walter chanced to meet up with skipper Colin Cross who asked him to come as sparehand aboard the *Kingston Turquoise* (H.50). On the spur of the moment, and because the skipper was a good friend, he went. Sadly, it turned out that this trawler was doomed. Perhaps one of the reasons Walter accepted a trip aboard the *Turquoise* was because he could take the family pet *Lassie* — as he had done on other trawlers. The dog often went wild and dashed around the ship after seagulls, or rolled about in the fish and slime while the men tried to gut. *Lassie* seemed as crazy an extrovert as her owner.

On 6th January, 1965, Dill joined the *Kingston Turquoise* for his second trip. Just before the crew sailed, one of the deckhands got married and Walter was amongst the guests at the wedding reception held at the Wassand Arms (Goulton Street). Some of the port's top skippers were also there, and no doubt Dillinger was his usual playful self.

Bad weather meant that the *Turquoise* had a poor trip to Iceland. By 25th January (around 1700 hours) the 811-ton trawler approached Scotland on her way home to Hull. Everything was quiet on the bridge where mate Bill Ward had just sighted and charted Brough Head Light (NW Orkney Island); Walter was at the wheel; deckie-learner John Seymour had gone down to the galley to get the others a mug of tea; and skipper Colin Cross had just come on to the bridge.

The Kingston trawler was doing 14-knots when there was a loud bang. First thoughts were that there had been an explosion in the engine-room; but it was soon realised that they had hit a reef. Unluckily, the *Kingston Turquoise* had struck "a needle in a haystack" — a sharp uncharted rock 14 miles off Hoyhead. The vessel began to sink fast (and was actually to go under within four minutes). The order was given to abandon ship. Mate Ward and Walter launched one of the inflatable life-rafts, while skipper Cross and deckie Seymour launched the other (they got into difficulties, but the young lad

This is George Lee of Blenheim Street (No.112 – c.1930s) with his extra large, hearse-like taxi – Dillinger's favourite cab-driver. George was born down Edinburgh Street and both his grandfathers were killed when washed overboard from Hull trawlers. He began taxying with a horse-drawn hansom cab. Daughter Brenda recalls that "many a time, I came downstairs to find a fisherman asleep in our kitchen because he was too drunk to go home".
Courtesy Brenda Simpson.

Rayners pub once had the longest bar in Hull. At the end nearest the 'gents', Dillinger and his mates gathered. The year is not known when this picture was taken, but the rosette suggests that it was a time when Hull F.C. got to the Rugby Final at Wembley. Some of these men, as far as is known, are Fred Casey (seated in the middle), Ginger Thompson, Charlie 'Chivers'(?), Chris Charlton, Harold 'Pat' Petrini, Freddie Fall, Dill with Pat's tie in his mouth, and an unidentified elderly man. Courtesy Harold Petrini.

The following story goes with this unidentified 1960s wedding photo. Apparently, the groom approached Dill in Rayners pub and asked him to act as best man (or witness?) at his wedding. Dill downed his pint and went along to the Hull Registry Office. Perhaps one day, this tale will be confirmed or denied by the couple who got married(?).
Courtesy Arthur Denton.

*The oil-burner **Kingston Turquoise** (H.50) was built by Cook, Welton & Gemmell of Beverley in 1955. This 811-ton trawler is seen here aground in the Humber on new Year's Eve 1959. A few years later, Dillinger was aboard this trawler (25th January 1965) when she struck an uncharted reef and sank off Hoyhead (Orkneys). He was the only crewman to lose his life, along with his dog **Lassie**.*
Courtesy Hull Daily Mail.

eventually put it right).

There was no time to lose as the vessel began to sink to the starboard (right) side. Still being propelled forward, the *Turquoise* arched around in a half circle as she gradually submerged, stern first. The crew divided into two groups on the boat-deck at the stern. All but one got into the life-rafts. The odd-man-out was, of course, Dillinger.

We can only guess what went through his mind at that vital moment. Dillinger was always a self-determined man who acted on his own initiative. He was never afraid to do anything out of the ordinary — especially under the shadow of death. In the past, his risky stunts had worked.

I believe that Dillinger dashed off to save his pet dog. Once he saw that his crewmates were getting safely into the life-rafts he had helped launch, his passionate heart went out to the forlorn creature. Just a couple of minutes before impact, well-trained *Lassie* scratched at the portside door of the wheelhouse to do her business outside on the deck. When Dill left the crew at the stern. it was along the *portside* that he ran. He not only wore a life-jacket, but had a life-belt too. As the ship heeled to starboard, he was seen to leap over the portside. He may or may not have had the animal in his arms.

I interviewed mate Bill Ward recently and he disagrees with my dog theory. As he was there at the time, he is obviously in a better position to judge what happened. He described Dillinger as a good swimmer and a knowledgeable mariner who knew the sea well. Bill believes that Dill was aware that the ship was quickly going down stern first and that it would drag the life-rafts under with it. He therefore left them at the stern, dashed along the portside, and leapt into the sea well clear of the vessel.

The difficulty was that the temperature of the water was barely above freezing (34/35 degrees Fahrenheit). With only his ordinary clothes on, Dillinger must have soon got cramp in his legs and was unable to swim. Some of the nineteen crewmen huddled in the two rafts saw Walter who was adrift about forty yards away. But they were unable to paddle to him to make a rescue. As he floated further away they heard him shout, "Hurry up lads, hurry up please". It was dusk and Walt was caught in a current which swept him away until he vanished behind a wave...

The immediate reaction of the Denton family, on being told of Walter's loss, was echoed by his son Arthur, "If he's mucking about, I'll kill 'im". Sarah who was very seriously ill (a long-time sufferer of Parkinson's Disease), knew her man was a powerful swimmer and believed in her heart he was still alive. She imagined he had got onto a reef, been picked up by a foreign trawler, and landed abroad in somewhere like Russia. For months the family hung onto the hope that Dill would knock on their front door with a broad grin on his face.

He never did.

Walter Denton's memorial service at the Fishermen's Bethel, led by Pastor Tom Chappell, was packed, and even overflowed outside. Everyone cried. Some of Walter's young cousins attended and one commented that she had never seen so many grown men and women full of tears. Above all their sobs, though, was the awful animal-like wail from Sarah at the front of the Bethel. She had recently had a major operation and was very weak. She was held

HELLYER BROS LIMITED

TELEPHONE :
26861 (6 LINES)

ST. ANDREWS DOCK
HULL

TELEGRAMS :
"ICEBERG, HULL"

TELEX No.
52162

5th February, 1965.

Mrs. W. Denton,
41, Harrow Street,
Hull.

Dear Mrs. Denton,

It was with great sorrow that we learned of the loss of your husband in such tragic circumstances in the sinking of the "Kingston Turquoise". Mr. Denton had served in this company's vessels for very many years, and I assure you he was held in high esteem by all who knew him.

Please accept our deepest and most heartfelt sympathy in your irreparable loss.

Yours sincerely,

This letter to Sarah Denton, signed by Graham Hellyer, needs no more words.
Courtesy Arthur Denton.

by her two sons, Billie and Arthur.

It was only later, at the official Inquiry into the loss of the *Kingston Turquoise*, that the truth hit the Denton family. This was not another of the famous Dillinger jokes — he *was* dead.

Dillinger died as he lived. He knew life was a risk, and so he lovingly embraced the danger of it, he revelled in it. Dill probably got the gambler's thrill from his cheeky defiance of Lady Fortune; but he flaunted her favours once too often.

Hessle Road is a poorer place for the loss of its dynamic son. A dare-devil yes, but as an Eton Street woman who knew the Dentons said, "For all his jokes, he was a fine man".

Dillinger would not want any story about himself to end on a sad note. This Christmas tale has a Robin-Hood-type twist, and illustrates that "if Dill felt sorry for someone, he'd help 'em in his own funny way". While going to Rayners one lunch-time, with his wife Sarah for a Yuletide drink, he saw an old woman near a butcher's display outside a Hessle Road shop. He boldly picked up two chickens, opened her large shopping bag, put them inside and said, "There's yer Christmas dinner, love".

REFERENCES

ANSON, Peter F. (1932) *Fishermen & Fishing Ways*, London: George G. Harrup & Co.

BARKER, Ralph (No Date) *The Blockade Busters*, London: Chatto & Windus.

BOCHEL, Margaret (1982) *The Fisher Lassies* in "*Odyssy*" edited by Billy Kay (Second Collection) Polygon Books, pp. 33-34.

CROWTHER, Ernest (1987) *Worse Things Happen at Sea: an autobiography of early life in Hull and a sea apprenticeship in the Merchant Navy*, Hull: Malet Lambert Local History Original. Volume 36.

DOUGLAS, J.D. (1962 — Organising Editor) *The New Bible Dictionary*, London: Inter-varsity Press.

FRAZER, Sir James (1922) *The Golden Bough: a Study in Magic and Religion*, (Abridged Edition) London: Macmillan/Papermac.

GILL, Alec (1987) *Hessle Road: A Photographer's View of Hull's Trawling Days*, Cherry Burton: Hutton Press.

GILL, Alec (1989) *Lost Trawlers of Hull: Nine Hundred Losses 1835-1987*, Cherry Burton: Hutton Press.

GILL, Alec & SARGEANT, Gary (1985) *Village Within A City: The Hessle Road Fishing Community of Hull*, Hull: University Press.

HOLLAND-MARTIN, Admiral Sir Deric (1969) *Trawler Safety: Final Report of the Committee of Inquiry into Trawler Safety*, London: H.M.S.O.

HOLY BIBLE, The (1978) *New International Version*, Grand Rapids, Michigan: Zondervan Bible Publishers.

HULL & YORKSHIRE TIMES 'There's a Catch in Their Knitting — We Hope!' 12 May 1962 (No.3265), p.1.

HULL TIMES 'Dramatic Rescue of Hull Trawler Crew' 22 April 1939, p.2.

OPIE, Iona & TATEM, Moira (1989) *A Dictionary of Superstitions*, Oxford: University Press.

PEARSON, Gordon (1974) 'Home from the Sea', *THE HUMBER LIGHT: Journal of the Hull & District Branch of the World Ship Society*, Volume 9 (1), January, pp. 13-15.

RADFORD, E. & M.A. (1975) *Encyclopedia of Superstitions*, Hutchinson.